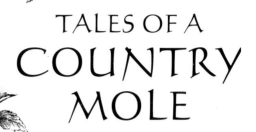

TALES OF A
COUNTRY
MOLE

by
Dorothy Rose

First Edition, 1997

Design and Layout, Robin Stevenson, Kairos Press.
Body text set in Goudy Old Style BT, 10.5pt.
Imagesetting by CDS Imaging, Leicester.
Printed in Great Britain by Norwood Press, Anstey, Leicester.

Cover & original drawings by Jacqui Bromley
Additional pictures from *Familiar Wild Flowers*, by F. Edward Hulme,
and *Wayside and Woodland Blossoms*, by Edward Step.

The Glory of the Garden by Rudyard Kipling is reproduced by permission of
A. P. Watt Ltd on behalf of The National Trust.
Source: *The Works of Rudyard Kipling* (1994) The Wordsworth Poetry Library

Kairos Press
552 Bradgate Road
Newtown Linford
Leicestershire   LE6 0HB
Great Britain

ACKNOWLEDGEMENTS

I am greatly endebted to all my family and friends who have helped to make this book possible. In particular I wish to thank Janet Welch, Elizabeth Waddel, Christopher Lee, Betty Dixon, Andrew Flower, Alison Mott and Jill Chandler.

4

All royalties from the sale of this book are to be divided equally between the following organisations:-

L O R O S
HOSPICE CARE FOR LEICESTERSHIRE

Groby Road, Leicester, LE3 9QE
Registered charity 506120

LOROS is a charity providing Hospice Care for patients throughout Leicestershire and Rutland who are terminally ill, mainly with cancer, and giving support to their families. In addition to the 25 in-patient unit at Groby Road, Leicester, LOROS has a day centre – Manor Croft – which takes up to 125 patients a week, a Home Care Team, a Lymphoedema Clinic, a Counselling Service, and a volunteer Home Sitting Service.

All LOROS services are provided free of charge to those in need

MULTIPLE SCLEROSIS SOCIETY
OF GREAT BRITAIN AND NORTHERN IRELAND
25 Effie Road, Fulham,
London SW6 1EE
Registered charity 207495

The Multiple Sclerosis Society is the nationwide organisation dedicated to supporting people with multiple sclerosis, providing the care they need in their everyday lives and supporting the research that is urgently required to understand this distressing disease.

Friends of
MOORFIELDS EYE HOSPITAL

162 City Road London EC1V 2PD
Registered charity 228637

Established in 1963 the Friends of Moorfields raises funds to provide valuable facilities and benefits for the Hospital and its patients. Money raised is applied in the first place towards the provision of services, amenities and equipment for the greater comfort and well-being of patients. Secondly money is used to purchase technical apparatus to promote new techniques for diagnosis and treatment of eye disease in the Hospital.

BRAIN RESEARCH FUND

Division of Clinical Neurology
QUEENS MEDICAL CENTRE
Nottingham

The Brain Research Fund is used to support research into degenerative diseases of the nervous system, including Alzheimer's disease, Parkinson's disease and motor neurone disease, with the aim of understanding the cause of brain damage in these conditions, and in the hope of finding a cure.

Contents

INTRODUCTION

You may be wondering how the tales of this Country Mole came to be "earthed up". As everyone knows the Mole is an earth mover, resilient and steadfast in its life's task to find the way through, and to get there no matter what unseen hazard comes in its pathway.

I too have always been a great gardener – more creative than the Mole, but like him, using my hands where many would use a fork. Helen, my daughter, was the creator of the actual name of *Mole*. When only a child she would come into my bedroom and stroke my face and say, "You are like a lovely soft velvety mole", and so I have been Mole for many years. Without the encouragement of my husband Eric, my daughter Helen, and that of many friends this book would not have been written.

One evening, whilst sitting in my fireside chair with friendly flames flickering in the fire, the peace and contentment I felt was in great contrast to the cold, hard realities of the possible war developing in the Gulf.

The local evening newspaper announced an appeal for the people of Leicestershire to support and encourage their very own 9/12 Royal Lancers Regiment serving out in the Gulf. A postal campaign was suggested. Without further hesitation I began to write letters each evening. My inner fire had been ignited and I wanted to reach out and touch the lives of these soldiers with human warmth and passion during this bleak time of their lives.

The words and stories flowed freely from my pen. Somehow I recalled a different story to each individual soldier, almost as if there was someone driving me on. This pen I used too, in spite of all the letters I wrote, seemed to go on and on without a refill.

Valentine's Day came along and again I set to work writing cards to as many soldiers as was possible including a card to Storming Norman Schwarzkoff to which he replied immediately even though he was at that time planning the final stages of the Desert Storm Campaign. Naturally I informed the local newspaper of this gesture. Immediately my photograph and a copy of the letter was printed in the evening papers. Also the ITV crew arrived and that very evening I appeared on the News.

When it came to the war in Bosnia, again the local newspaper recruited me to encourage the Leicester people to pick up their pens and write once more to these soldiers. Again I appeared on ITV, being proclaimed as a prolific writer once more.

So at last I realised that the many stories I had written during these war years should be recorded in a book.

Like my counterpart the Mole, I have reached my goal.

one
EARLY DAYS

*R*ose Bell and David Cook were both twenty years of age when they married on November 24th in the year 1895, before the altar of the Wesleyan Methodist Chapel in Horncastle a small market town in Lincolnshire.

They were a handsome couple, she with her beautiful long raven black hair and dark brown eyes typical of the Romany Clan who settled in and around Lincolnshire, he with his fair gingery hair and moustache and blue eyes. People remarked upon their striking appearance and welcomed them warmly to the community.

David's father William was a travelling grocer. He sold his produce from an open dray drawn by his faithful horse Dobbin. To protect his goods against the rain and snow he used large mackintosh sheets. He also needed protection for himself from the biting winds which are renowned across the Lincolnshire Wolds. It was indeed a long day for him, riding wherever possible on the shafts of the dray, as he journeyed to all the outlying hamlets, having to negotiate small bumpy lanes in order to reach his valued customers who depended upon him and his varied wares. The housewives looked forward to his weekly visits to replenish their stocks of candles, lamp wicks and glasses, matches and paraffin, enamel utensils, knicker elastic, Germaline ointment and all those little things that mean so much. On arriving home his work was still not finished until his faithful horse had been groomed and fed before he could relax and enjoy his own evening meal.

Quite a contrast was Rose Bell's father Will, who was a master brewer. He too worked hard and long hours often from five in the morning until dusk. Unlike William who had to endure the elements Will enjoyed the warm aromatic atmosphere of the brewery. He made full use of British malt and hops in the brewing of beer, a labour intensive process unlike the mechanisation used today. Each brewing required a period of four to five weeks for the processes of fermentation and germination to take place before it was ready for sale. This was an anxious period for him because an unsuccessful brew meant hard times until his next batch was complete.

David was very fortunate to have a father like William who established him in both a greengrocery and grocery shop in a little side street in Horncastle. This was to be his wedding present, meanwhile Rose Bell's father who was interested in carpentry made them an oak chest of drawers, four chairs and a Pembroke table. The table is still in everyday use and is in very good condition – not a sign of a worm anywhere.

David and his father William always looked forward to the Annual Horse Fair which was held every August in Horncastle and noted for being one of the largest fairs in the world in the Nineteenth Century. Gypsies travelled from all parts of the country to buy and sell horses.

Although David's roots were here in this little attractive town, the sight of the beautifully groomed horses with shining harnesses being paraded on the cobbled market place stirred a great longing within him. He just loved horses and his greatest dream was to make a home for himself and his beloved Rose Bell somewhere in the countryside.

Within the first two years of their marriage two sons were born, the elder called William, the younger one Jack.

Although the small grocers shop brought in a sufficient livelihood to provide for David and his family he was often very restless, knowing that this was not the life for him, and he could not shut away the craving for the countryside.

After school was over for the day the children would clamber into the shop clutching their farthings or if they were lucky even a half-penny. They would stand and stare at the contents of the big glass jars as they stood on the shelves, before making a choice. Some of the parents marvelled at William and Jack who never pestered their mother and father for any of the sweets. One of them said to David, "How is it your boys never demand any of the sweets?" To which David replied that at first he let them loose in the shop to eat as many sweets as they so desired. The nature of children being what it is William and Jack gorged themselves on the goodies. Eventually they were unwell and violently sick and after this incident there was never reason to scold them for helping themselves.

On a Wednesday afternoon when the shop was closed David would get out his bicycle and travel from village to village looking for the house and farm of his dreams. So it was no wonder that when he entered the village of Kirkby-on-Bain he was just spellbound. At first he was attracted by the old Mill House, with its old mill wheel churning the frothy water into the mill pool. He cycled on and came across the village store, went in and enquired if there were any farms for sale. As it so happened it was to be his lucky day – the shop keeper informed him that the farm next to her property was up for sale. The first thing he noticed was the name of Linden Farm up on the field gate. Although the house was quite small he was attracted by the large farmyard and farm buildings, some of which were in disrepair. Still he was undaunted, went through the farm gate and knocked on the door. He stated his business and was invited in by a very comely woman. She called her husband and soon he and David got down to discussing the price and when the property would be vacant. There was just one problem he had to solve and that was to sell the shop and house in Horncastle. The farmer agreed to wait a few weeks to give David time to negotiate a sale of his property. My! how the wheels of his old bicycle revolved on his return journey to Horncastle to break the good news to Rose Bell. The weeks that lay ahead were very anxious ones. Oh! how he wished that he could soon find a customer for his business.

David right from a child had a certain keenness about him, to the extent that his father had high hopes of him becoming an auctioneer and had already made arrangements for him to be articled in a firm of local auctioneers. But alas! on the very night that his fate would have been sealed David played a stupid prank causing his father both disappointment and disillusionment. Although David was sixteen years old at the time, his prank was not appreciated either by his parents or indeed their neighbours. He had spent his pocket money on small bombs in which one inserted a cap. These he tied to the door handle of each terraced cottage and as the resident opened the door the bomb hit the ground and went bang. David's father immediately cancelled his apprenticeship and set him to work in the shop. Sad to say he would have made a very good auctioneer as he had what is commonly called the "gift of the gab" and never stopped talking.

This gift of his now proved very fruitful, as he was not long in persuading a man and his family that the shop and house would indeed make them a very viable property. Luckily too, David's father intended retiring and gave David the old Dray horse which was a great help in moving the family as well as the furniture and effects to Linden Farm. By this time there was another mouth to feed; Rose Bell had given birth to a daughter who they christened Daisy.

When the two boys William and Jack saw the open fields and barns they gave Rose Bell very little trouble. Times were hard for both David and Rose Bell and they had to work long hours, firstly to get the house in order. One day one of the villagers was chatting to David and asked him if he would like to earn some extra cash. Living in a very big house nearby was a family who had an elderly parent living with them who needed someone to keep an eye on him during the night. This was a wonderful opportunity for David. He went along and was accepted and for these services he was paid good money.

Consequently he was able to buy his first cow. But he had never milked a cow before so had to ask the help of one of the local farmers. At least they would have milk and butter for the family.

People in the village were very kind. One farmer loaned him a plough and so his old horse Dobbin was harnessed to it, and this too was a new experience for both David and horse.

That winter David laid one field to wheat. Gradually things began to take shape. Next on the list were a few chickens which roamed around the farmyard and the two boys enjoyed looking for the eggs.

Meanwhile David got down to repairing the barns as best he could with what spare cash he had from his night job. He would snatch a few hours sleep during the day as he knew he had no choice but to work hard to achieve his object of making a good life for himself and his family. At times Rose Bell must have been too exhausted to even wonder if they had made the right decision. Still on they struggled hoping for better days. But, oh dear! Once again Rose Bell was pregnant. The country air seemed to suit their constitutions. Rose Bell flourished and in every way proved to be a real "earth mother". Whether it was the country air or the earth they stood on could not be guessed. The fields gave the harvest, the trees their fruit and Rose Bell herself was just fruitful of womb. Then one day luck was on their side. David won the pig at skittles at the Garden Fete. It was rumoured that the organisers had planned that David should be the winner as his need was great at this time.

David's first impressions of his chosen village were to be proved right. It had a warm welcoming feel about it with the evocative sounds of the blacksmith and delivery people going about their daily work. Each one an amusing character, a part of the jigsaw that made up the community.

Slowly David and Rose Bell joined in the local community and it was not long before they realised that this was not only a pretty little village but that it had an interesting history. For instance the impressive school clock and bell were given by a Captain Wilson in 1871 the inscription on the bell being "Presented to Kirkby-on-Bain Primary School".

Captain Robert Wilson was a director of the Shipping Line named Wilson Liners. It is said that the clock came from one of these liners but it was hardly likely because of the pendulum movement – not the kind of clock to be used on a liner tossing in the high seas.

In a quiet corner of the village was the church yard and lovely old church. Although money was donated by Queen Anne in 1712 for the erection of this church it was given the name of St. Mary. Strange really that it was not named after the queen who was the main benefactor.

The Pub was called the Ebrington Arms. This was built way back in 1582 and was originally owned by (well of course!) the Ebrington family who were landowners in Lincolnshire. In later years they moved to Devon and bought another pub and called it the Ebrington Arms. At one time these two pubs were the only ones with such a name in the whole of the country. It seems landowners and publicans make a good partnership. No doubt they were fond of a tipple or two.

During my life time the Post Office has moved to three different properties. When I was a child it was in a semi-detached house on a corner of the main street. It was a very small room at the front with a very large counter. The letter box was in the wall. This one was owned by an elderly gentleman called Mr Marshall. In fact he looked very much like Pickwick in Pickwick Papers by Charles Dickens. I still possess an old ivory paper knife he gave to me dated 1895, on which are inscribed the dates and months of that year.

The Blacksmith was an unusual character in his old tatty leather apron with its big pocket. Like most blacksmiths he was big and strong, tall and broadly built. But he was what is spoken of as "Deaf as a door nail". When he was shoeing a horse if the animal became a little restless one could hear him bellowing out "Wow Wow". In fact if the horse had not been tethered then I am convinced he would have galloped out of the open doors in fright. But it was very fascinating to go into his shop and watch the glow of the flames as the bellows were pumped to heat the shoes for the horses and for making other items required by the villagers. The very hot shoes and implements were removed from the heat and were shaped on the anvil, the noise of which could be heard as the blacksmith hammered away. Once they were ready they were immersed in a bath of cold water and believe me a lot of sizzling and steaming took place. If he dropped anything you would hear him say "Dang the thing" and not damn. This was only natural as he was the Lay Preacher of the Wesleyan Chapel. But no doubt it was thirsty work and every Saturday night he could be seen taking his pint jug to be filled at the back door of the pub.

The same applied to the Lay Preacher of the Primitive Chapel. He would talk to us in Sunday School of the wickedness of drinking beer and spirits and ask us to sign the pledge that we would never partake of these evil drinks. Yet he too would take his pint jug to be filled at the back door of the pub every Saturday night. One wonders if they felt it less wicked to obtain their beer at the back door and to take it home to drink rather than to enter by the main entrance.

Jackie Sharp was the village carpenter and undertaker and also the Verger at the Church. He would toll the one and only bell, calling the Parishioners to Church every Sunday morning and evening and on Good Friday. If there was a death in the village the way he rang the bell denoted to the parishioners whether it was male or female. When the Second World War broke out he would also toll the bell for the All Clear. After 50 years I still use the rolling pin he gave to me as a wedding present. Every Sunday morning he would be seen entering the school to wind the clock before taking up his duties as Sexton at the Church. He was a very active man and did not retire until he was eighty years old.

There was a Chimney Sweep named Bill Thornley and even as a child I was fascinated by him. He was such a strange character, he spoke very broad Lincolnshire. With his bag of brushes he would knock at the door and then walk straight in shouting "Aye yer ready fomme missus?" All the time he was sweeping the chimney his nose would be running and he would be chattering away to himself. When the job was done and he had accepted his payment of 2/6 from Rose Bell he always said, "I have not made you much muck missus". That was his opinion. The fact that she may have spent the rest of the morning cleaning away soot from all the surfaces in the room proved that a housewife had other ideas of how much muck was acceptable.

The village shop was owned by a lady named Mrs Pinning. Now there was an unusual tale about her. Although she was not regularly a gambling woman she always placed a bet on a horse running in the Lincolnshire Handicap. But on the eve of the race she told everyone that her bet would not be placed until the morning. Indeed you may ask why? Well, as the story goes she always had a dream and strange though it may seem she always had an uncanny message or premonition giving a hint of the name of the winning horse. It remained an unsolved mystery as to how anyone could ever dream the name of a winning horse in just this one race.

Mrs Pinning also made news when she refused to pay her water rates. Her reason for this was because the farmers in the outlying farms were exempt from any charge, although their water drained into the village. Eventually she was warned that if she still refused to pay the bailiffs would move in. Her immediate reply to this was to barricade all doors and goods were sold through a hatch which she had had made in the shop door. After a time she sold the premises and purchased a shop in Horncastle. Naturally, she thought her debt was forgotten but she was very much mistaken and the bailiffs walked in and demanded money or goods, so at last they caught up with her.

Although one could purchase most things in the village shop, every Monday morning a little old gentleman could be seen called Honest John pushing his wooden truck through the village selling his wares. In all weathers he made this journey from Horncastle, a matter of five miles. He had a very good selection of items suitable to the requirements of every household, i.e. black and white elastic, ribbons in all colours and widths, wool for darning socks, buttons, press studs, needles and pins and reels of cotton. He also made sure he had a good supply of Snowfire aboard. This was a very good cream in the shape of a small round block and ideal for chapped hands and was very popular with the housewives.

It seems incredible that in twenty one years Rose Bell gave birth to twelve children. There was little wonder that when the number reached seven their little cottage was bursting at the seams. David had no other choice but to consider selling Linden Farm and to look for another property. "Lady Luck" once more came his way. A farm nearby had a sign on the main gate but, "To Let Only". He jumped at the chance of this. Went to see the owners and was accepted as tenant. With the sale of Linden Cottage it meant he could invest his money in many other ways. His first purchase was a pony and "Tub" trap for Rose Bell, whereby she too could earn extra money by taking people to the doctors' surgery at both Woodhall Spa and Coningsby. At times she would collect medicine for them and if I was really good she would take me along at night time. Bonny the pony was backed into the shafts, new candles were placed into the carriage lamps which were positioned each side of the trap, I was warmly wrapped in the trap blanket and away we went.

Rose Bell, with Daisy and Lily, and Bonny the pony.

David had always been a lover of horses and so it seems hardly possible that to earn extra money he purchased young horses and schooled them in readiness to be sent to France to help in the war effort and to perhaps be killed.

Still, times were hard. For instance the Government clamped down on all farmers to forfeit all the corn they produced. If anyone was found hiding any, then a heavy fine was imposed. It was only natural that all the farmers retained a little for their hens which had to be secretly fed to them.

When David had his shop in Horncastle he would buy treacle by the barrel and sell it loose. He decided to purchase one now and he soon had many customers, providing another small addition to the family income.

In the early morning of 17th October 1917 the silence of this sleepy little village was broken by the crowing of the farmyard cockerel and in the distance could be heard the faint hooting of the owl as he flew off after his night's vigil in the trees in the churchyard which was adjacent to the farmhouse and buildings. They were unaware that in the farmhouse Rose Bell also began to stir when she became aware that very soon she would give birth to her baby. David was awakened from his slumbers to go and fetch the Village Midwife. On returning he quickly made a coal fire in the living room to get hot water to the ready. By now he knew well what he was expected to do having previously attended Rose Bell at the births of the eleven other children.

Very soon there was a cry from the bedroom and David was told he was the father of yet another daughter.

As time passed by naturally a name had to be decided upon for this new born baby. As before my mother, Rose Bell, favoured a flower name, consequently her choice was that of her own – just Rose. David, my father, meanwhile thought hard and long, he wanted a name beginning with the letter D and so it was that he chose Dorothy as my first Christian name. One of the Godmothers was a young girl called Mitt Peters. She and her parents were refugees from Belgium living in the village. Apparently Mitt was so delighted to be a Godmother to an English child. After the War they moved back to Antwerp but for many years kept in touch at Christmas time.

Mitt Peters, Dorothy Rose's godmother, in a photograph taken some years later.

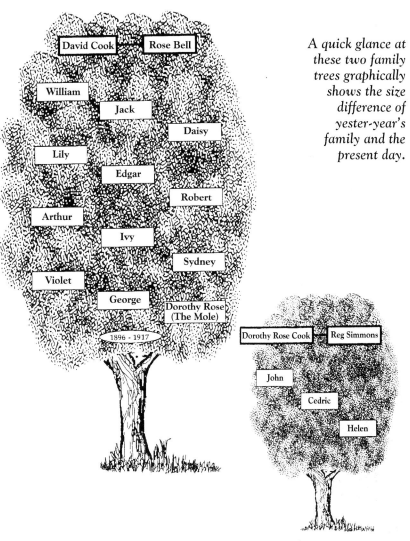

A *quick glance at these two family trees graphically shows the size difference of yester-year's family and the present day.*

Many generations of the Cook and Bell families resided in Horncastle and can be traced back to 1728. The first recorded instance of the name Cook occurs in the writs of Parliament where one Emma Cook from Norfolk and one Roger le Cook from Yorkshire were registered therein. Notable bearers of the name include James Cook (1728-1779) the English explorer who commanded expeditions to the South Pacific on the ships 'Resolution', 'Adventure' and 'Endeavour'.

There are several possible explanations for the origin of the English surname of Bell. In the first instance the name may be of Matronymic origin derived from the first name of a mother. Also the name may be a pet-form of Isabel, Spanish and Southern French form of Elizabeth. Early instances of the name date from 1086 when the Domesday Book was compiled. One Filius Belli of Suffolk was recorded therein. The name may also be considered local in origin, belonging to that category of names derived from the place where a man once dwelt or held land. The name came to denote a dweller at the sign of the 'bell' or one who lived near the town bell.

As you can imagine being part of such a large family had its many ups and downs. The boys were inclined to be jealous of the girls because they got on well together and were favoured by father. The girls helped with domestic chores and could interest themselves with hobbies such as needlework and embroidery, whereas the boys became restless and wanted to travel further a field. There was little for them in the village other than to offer their services to the British Army, consequently William and Jack finished up in France. The army was to figure greatly in the lives of all the male members of the family except Sydney.

Robert, who had to endure the middle name of Baden because it was a pre-condition of a ten pound gift offered by a daily paper eager to commemorate in 1908 the founding of the Boy Scout movement in Great Britain, was also a member of the army and was later sent out to India and suffered with malaria.

Tragedy struck the family in 1920 following the great flood of Louth. It was on May 29th 1920, called "Black Saturday", that an appalling avalanche of water suddenly descended without warning on the market town of Louth which is situated in a valley at the foot of the Lincolnshire Wolds. All movable objects in its path were swept along – animals, cars, carts and trees. It was estimated that 7.5 million tons of water passed through the Bridge gap in Bridge Street, causing buildings to collapse.

The torrents raged through the villages including Kirkby-on-Bain. The River Bain was bursting its banks. Sadly my brother Sidney along with some of the village boys decided to go swimming unknown to their parents. Suddenly Sidney was washed away and was not found until a few days later when the water subsided. This was the first victim that the River Bain claimed.

Although I was only three years old at this time, and too young to understand the tragic circumstances of this accident, in later years I realised what a great shock it was to both my parents especially to my mother who was in bed with Rheumatic Fever and too ill to attend her little lad's funeral. In fact the whole village was in a state of shock, being such a close community.

Sydney Cook

19

Daisy was the first of the girls. She was petite, rather like the carefree daisies growing in the fields. She became a mother's help in a well-to-do house in Horncastle. She met and married a soldier after the First World War. She had two sons but when they were quite young her husband died from the effects of the war. She struggled on to bring up the boys with the help of relatives.

Lily came next. She was tall and slender with all the elegance and countenance of her flower namesake. She went to London and became a Hairdresser. At the age of nineteen she married Billy, the youngest son of a family named Taylor. In fact Rose Bell's sister, also called Lily, married Arthur, the eldest son of this same family. Now these two brothers, Arthur and Billy, were for many years the Valets and Chauffeurs to a Gentleman in Waiting to King George V. His name was Lord Armitage and he lived in a beautiful house in Cranford, Middlesex. When he retired he gave the two brothers a gold pocket watch each. After their retirement they became Book-Makers but sadly their watches were stolen on one of their visits to the Greyhound Stadium at Wembley.

Ivy, another flower name chosen by Rose Bell was a comely, rather independent girl. She decided to take up nursing and off she went to London to do her training in a hospital there. Sadly she died when only twenty-two years old. She would cycle from her digs to the hospital and on one particular journey just before she was due to come home for Christmas, the rain just poured down. Consequently she was very wet and stayed on duty in wet clothes. For ten days she was extremely ill. David and Rose Bell were sent for but she never recovered. Both were very sad when they returned to Reddings Farm. I still remember Rose Bell's white and sad face as she entered the home.

Violet came next. Just like a spring Violet, shy but with a remarkable beauty in her face which was framed by golden red hair, the texture of sable. She was always very frail and remained at home. She too died at the tender age of eighteen years.

Finally, came the Briar Rose or otherwise Dorothy Rose, whose vigorous outgoing nature made a stark contrast with her rose petal complexion and sparkling brown eyes. The birth of Dorothy Rose made a total of twelve children to be borne of Rose Bell. None of the family took after her in producing such a large family.

When I was just three years old my father David left Lockwood Farm and bought a beautiful mud and stud white washed cottage with a thatched roof on Wharf Road which led to the river.

Strange though it may seem this cottage was known as Rose Cottage but for business reasons David changed the name to Reddings Farm. He had already acquired a field on a hillside along the lane towards Woodhall Spa which was always known as Reddings Hill and the spinney running alongside was named Reddings Wood. No doubt the name Reddings appealed to him and for the rest of his life he lived at Reddings Farm.

The cottage and farm buildings and crew yard stood in about five acres of land with the River Bain running through the fields. Many oak trees must have been felled when the cottage was built. As you entered the rooms all the beams were exposed and in beautiful condition with no sign of woodworm.

The back door to the property opened straight into the kitchen, where stood the big old pine wash stand on which were two white enamel bowls for washing up. Underneath the stand were buckets of water from the pump or rain water butts. Every drop of water had to be carried into the house. At one time this kitchen had been much bigger but half of it had been boarded off to gain another bedroom.

The main flight of stairs went up from a door out of the kitchen straight into the first bedroom. Believe me no one could go up or down those stairs without being heard. Each stair had its own creak – not to be wondered at when you think of the years of service those stairs had provided for many families. From the kitchen a door led into the living room with its cosy old black leaded Victorian cooking stove, boiler on one side of the fire and the oven on the opposite side. The boiler would take at least three buckets of water which would quickly heat up for general use. This had to be constantly topped up. There was what was called a 'Tidy' in the front of the coal fire, which obscured the ashes from view. Surrounding the whole of the hearth was the big iron fender with its shiny steel rim, complete with long handled steel poker and shovel.

In the centre of the room was the much used pine table which when not in use was covered with a colourful velvety cloth with tassels all round it. An ideal attraction for the cats. The main furniture was a chaise longue commonly called a couch and two matching chairs, all covered in green leather but now very faded after years of wear. In front of one window stood a table with the radio on top and its accumulator battery. The battery was exchanged weekly to be renewed at a cost of sixpence per battery.

In the corner of this room was a small wall cupboard which housed condiments, sugar and flour. On one wall stood an old pine cupboard which was used for storing household linen, cloths for repairing etc. From the side of this room a door opened on to three steps which led down into a large cool dairy. The floors in the kitchen and living room were red brick. These were scrubbed regularly and when dry, pegged rugs were put down. These rugs were made out of clothes no longer fit for use, and cut into small strips to be threaded through a hessian base with a special tool. The hessian was mainly corn bags that had the seams unpicked, which were washed and cut to whatever size was required. These rugs were made by the women in the house and were very attractive. Colourful pieces of cloth were chosen for the centre piece and the four corners. Usually the border was black or navy and the remainder was multi-coloured.

The pictures which hung each side of the fireplace were a pleasure to look at. The frames were mahogany and on each one was printed "An Evening with Van Dyke". In one was a grand piano around which stood handsome men and women, no doubt having a sing-song, dressed in most beautiful attire with glasses of wine in their hands.

The living room was furnished with elaborately carved furniture and had gorgeous curtains up at the window. As you opened the door from this room you were immediately entering the sitting room or what was commonly called the front room. In front of the window was an old oak Pembroke Table made by Rose Bell's father which is still in the family today in good condition. There was an old piano kept only as a piece of furniture, some of the notes were broken. It had been handled by twelve children so there is no wonder very little tune was now gained from it.

There were six dining type chairs, a chaise longue or couch, a father's chair with arms, and a mother's chair without arms, allowing for the bustles on the dress, also for sewing, knitting, crochet or tatting with ease.

On the mantel shelf over the long black iron fireplace stood a mahogany, very narrow, glass case with sliding doors. In it were numerous china pieces. Apparently every time Rose Bell gave birth to a baby, David gave her a piece of china. When I was born he gave to her two vases on which were painted pretty pink roses. At the time they were full of chocolates. In one corner of the room was a small table on which stood the old gramophone and records. To complete the room two large pictures hung on the walls. They had oak frames with carved acorns in each corner. One was called Sun-Rise and the other Sun-Set. The sun-rise depicted lovely scenery with long horned cows drinking at the water's edge, whereas the sun-set depicted equally lovely scenery but with the cows either standing or some lying down chewing their cud and settling down for the night.

Strange though it may seem, the front door into the cottage went off from this room but at the back of the house. Also from this room another door led to the second flight of stairs to the bedroom occupied by George. This was indeed an amazing room. The oak beams were inset in the walls all round the room, about twelve inches from the floor. Straight ahead was the incredible chimney stack, right up to the roof, beautifully built in narrow bricks tapering upwards. On this hung a huge picture of King George V and Queen Mary both elegantly dressed.

High up over the bed two beams straddled the room about six feet apart. George and I had great fun swinging backwards and forwards on these two beams. We were like two performing monkeys. If we had a fall then we had a happy landing on the bed below. Again the furniture was pine, it was what was classed in those days as the poor man's furniture, but is today held in high esteem. There was a fine wash stand on which stood the old Victorian jug and bowl with two chamber pots on the shelf below. The dressing table had two narrow drawers only, with its matching cheval mirror. A cane bottomed chair each side of the bed completed the room.

The middle bedroom could only be approached by either of the other two bedrooms. So from George's bedroom you had to negotiate a step, then climb over one beam on to a step the other side before reaching the door to my room.

I loved the old maple wood double bed, with matching dressing table and wash stand. The large picture on the wall above my bed was of Flora MacDonald in a beautiful long green velvet gown, and Bonnie Prince Charlie looking so handsome. I spent many happy moments looking at these two people. Again beams protruded from all angles of the room.

Next came Rose Bell and Davids' room. To get into this bedroom I had to stride over a huge beam, the door was above this beam right up to the ceiling. Very strange indeed but very cute.

The furniture in this room was mahogany except the bed which was black iron with fancy brass trimmings. The chest of drawers was rather large with three deep drawers and two half drawers at the top. In one corner stood the kidney shaped wash stand with its marble top, with another jug and bowl, and soap dish and two chamber pots. The dressing table was quite simple but elegant with its two inlaid drawers and turned legs complete with a cheval mirror.

None of the bedrooms could accommodate a wardrobe so a rail was put up where the height of the room allowed, and a curtain was fixed to draw across to protect the clothes. The previously mentioned stairs led off from this room. There were only two small pictures in this room. A print of the Blue Boy and of Innocence, both in white frames. Rose Bell had a small table at the side of her bed and David a cane bottomed chair.

To make his small holding more viable David purchased further fields on the Moor Lane towards Woodhall Spa. Over the years the property had changed hands many times, but David always insisted that the deeds showed it was built in the 1600's by the Earl of Lovelace and given to his daughter, on her marriage to one of the wealthy Fortescue family who resided at Coningsby some three miles away.

Even though the cottage had to be cleaned and everything was topsy turvy for a while, I felt very happy there. Perhaps the low ceilings gave it more of a family atmosphere. At Lockwood Farm the ceilings were very high. My bedroom was the middle room and I felt very snug and safe with my parent's bedroom on one side and my brothers' bedroom on the other side.

Reddings Farm

Once my father had helped my mother to get the cottage straight he worked on the outbuildings. In my own little way I tried to help him by holding the nails as he repaired these buildings. He and I would feed the chickens but when it came to collecting the eggs he would watch me very carefully as I placed an egg into the bucket. It was obvious he was waiting for me to drop one.

One day he pulled out a big drawer from a very large wooden box and put in lots of eggs. To me this seemed a bit odd, I was so used to seeing my mother putting the clean clothes into drawers in the bedrooms. A paraffin lamp was also put into one end of this box to warm it up. Another funny thing happened, David was watching a red line in a piece of wood which was covered in glass and when it reached a certain place in the wood he shut the drawer. Day after day I watched him turning the eggs over. Oh! It just did not make sense. As the days went past I could not make it all out. Then one morning he sprinkled the eggs with water almost like a magician flicking his fingers here and there but still nothing happened. At least when mother ironed and sprinkled water on the clothes the heat of the iron sent some steam into the air.

Yet another day the eggs were sprinkled with water but nothing happened and the drawer was shut. But the next morning when David opened the drawer I looked in wonderment. I clapped my hands and jumped up and down, to see the shells cracking and lovely little chicks popping their heads out of the shells. At last I knew the answer to the long wait of so many eggs in one drawer in a large box. As the years rolled on I soon learned the name of incubator.

After all this David said to me "Come with me to ask your mother to make some food for the chicks". Whereupon Rose Bell put some eggs in a saucepan of water to boil on the fire but they took a long time because they had to be hard-boiled. Meanwhile she fetched a big bowl and a sieve and a loaf of bread. The crusts were cut off the loaf and she broke the loaf up into small pieces and started to sieve them. I knew that the pigs would get the bread crusts in their food so I had a good nibble before they went into the pig bucket.

Naturally I wanted a sieve and pointed to the tea strainer. My mother put it on the table and then fetched me a basin. I tried so hard but my crumbs were lumpy. Anyway my mother tipped them in with hers, beat up the eggs and mixed it all together. This tasted better than the crusts. I had my fill of egg and bread crumbs before it was taken for the chicks.

Meanwhile David had prepared the brooder and made sure it was warm from the paraffin lamp before putting in the chicks. What you don't really understand when so young is that the chicks know how to eat and drink without a mother there to show them. David reared such pretty chicks which soon grew into beautiful pullets and when around six months old would start laying eggs.

Once they reached this age David would advertise them for sale in the Feathered World and Poultry World and dispatch them to all parts of the country. He reared many breeds, one of the more elegant looking birds was the Leghorn, tall and stately with lovely white plumage, no wonder it is a star of children's cartoons. Each variety sported a distinctive name to match its dazzling feathers and striking comb and wattle. Unfortunately breeds such as the Blue Barred Plymouth Rocks, Black Minorcas, Blue Andalusians, Houdans, Dorkings and the Anconas are rarely to be seen in this day and age. The cockerels were a spectacular sight to be seen with their fan like tails strutting about, proud and sure of their own importance.

Black Minorcas   *Dorkings*

Sometimes David would fetch Tom the pony from the field across the river. He put a halter around his neck and lifted me onto his back. I hung on to his mane as we crossed over the river on a rocky old bridge. Some years later the river became very high and took this bridge away down stream, so David had to have a new one erected which felt much safer.

There were rabbits in this field over by the river and one day David thought he saw one under one of the chicken houses. He fetched his gun and shot at it. But he had a shock when he went to pick it up. He had shot one of his chickens by mistake.

Many times I watched my mother making butter so one day I went to the wood shed and found a little board and two pieces of wood for butter pats. I mixed some soil with water and made my own special mud butter with fancy markings on the top just like Mother's.

Some of the older girls had play-houses so I asked if I could have one. My father soon fixed it up. He gave me a little brick shed next to his kitchen garden and best of all made a little table and two stools. Rose Bell gave me a red mug and a few pieces of pottery. I had a pretty painted tin tea service and tray that Santa Claus had brought me that Christmas along with a cooker with little saucepans on top. It was lovely playing in my own little house with my dolls and two little black kittens.

For years I have remembered the day on which I was really very naughty. I dressed the two kittens in my dolls clothes and wanted them to lie on their backs in the pram. Of course they would not do so and so I smacked them and somehow caught the nose of one of them and made it bleed, this made me feel really upset so I picked it up and held it close to me to love it better; just like Mother did if I was hurt.

When I was four years old I should have been going to the woods for a picnic and to pick some primroses with the older children and our teacher. But I had the measles and felt really poorly. Out came the small folding iron bed and mother made me comfy in front of the fire in the living room. For years I was teased because it seems I had said to my mother "I don't mind not going to the woods if you will let me have my kattens in bed with me". How was I to know at that age that it should be kittens.

My brother George, being older than me, preferred to play with his pals. But on Saturday night, which was bath night, we played together. David would go to the pub at about 8 o'clock then out would come the wooden wash tub that Rose Bell used on wash days. This was filled with hot water from the boiler at the side of the fire and cooled with rain water from a bucket. We took it in turns to have the first bath. Once we had our clean pyjamas on and had our cup of cocoa we settled down to our musical evening.

George would get out the round biscuit tin and two wooden spoons and play the drums whilst I used a piece of grease-proof paper on a comb as a mouth organ. When we tired of this Rose Bell would play some records on the old gramophone while we nursed the kittens. Our mother would often glance at the clock and when it was nearing the time of our father's return from the pub she would make me a mug of cocoa and fill the stone hot water bottle for George's bed. She knew that I liked the oven shelf covered in brown paper for my bed. On hearing our father's footsteps mother carried up the lighted candles and we quickly followed her upstairs and crept into bed knowing we must be very quiet.

My first debut on the stage was when I was just four years old. My father had made a mock step out of timber and this was put on to the stage. Holding some bread and jam in my hands I walked to the middle of the stage and sat on this step. I had been taught to say

> I am sitting on the door step
> Eating bread and jam
> I ain't a really crying
> But I specs you think I am

I nearly did cry anyway with everyone looking at me. Later on in the evening I also recited the following:

If only it were Summer time
I know what I would do
I'd wander through the fields
And take my dollies too

Children at this age are either shy or very out-going. I enjoyed every minute of being on stage. I was also well applauded and felt very pleased with myself.

Once a year a small circus came to the village. It was held in the paddock next to my home. There were pretty girls on horseback, performing monkeys, and clowns up to their tricks. But it was frightening when the man came into the ring with snakes curling around his body. The circus only stayed one night and I was glad when they left. The snakes were too near to my home and I was almost too afraid to go to sleep that night in case one came into my bedroom.

In May of every year the children who attended the Wesleyan Sunday School were taken on an outing to Woodhall Spa. Wagons and horses were loaned for these occasions. Along with the Sunday School teachers we decorated the wagons with branches from the Laburnum trees, the yellow of the flowers standing out so vividly. Forms would be put into the wagons for sitting on whilst we travelled along. For these occasions my sister Lily would send me a brand new dress and hat to match. Once we reached Woodhall Spa we walked from street to street singing as we went along and making a collection in aid of Chapel funds. Before leaving for home we were taken to buy ice-creams.

Tea was prepared for our return at the Chapel. There was bread and butter and jam, plum loaf and seed cake with tea or lemonade. I decided to try a piece of seed cake. It was awful but I dare not leave it on my plate so I waited until no-one was looking and threw it well away from my place under the table. Fortunately the table cloths almost touched the floor so no-one could find out who the culprit was.

In the evening sports were held in one of my father's fields. He was chief organiser of the races. There were sack races, egg and spoon races, races for different age groups and so on. If you won you were given sixpence which was a lot of money in those days.

Just before Christmas a service was held in the Wesleyan Chapel and for good attendance at Sunday School we were given a reading book, a bag of sweets, an apple and an orange. One book I had was called "What Katy Did at School". In those days it always seemed to snow as we all left the Chapel with our parents to return home. Somehow we had a lovely warm feeling inside of us as we clutched our precious gifts. Mother would be busy icing the Christmas Cake and making mince pies. We knew that we had not long to wait for Santa Claus.

One day Father went to the railway station and brought back a huge cardboard box. Both George and I were sent into the living room and told to keep the door shut. Mother kept going upstairs, we could hear the stairs creaking. My brother George and I made a plan. That night I lit my candle, crept into his room and called him. Then we quietly entered my parent's bedroom and opened the boxes hiding behind my mother's chest of drawers. There were beautiful toy soldiers, a steam roller, a doll in a cot with lots of clothes for the doll and many other toys. That night George and I stayed awake to wait for Santa but who should enter the bedroom but my mother. This was the end of our dream. Sad though it may have been at the time it is a stage in life we all experience.

Naturally when someone tells you not to look or do something then you do just the opposite. The following story is typical of any child.

One day my mother asked me to fetch something out of one of the deep drawers in the very large chest of drawers but insisted that I was not to look into either of the two smaller drawers at the top. Curiosity killed the cat and I just could not wait for the opportunity to explore these two drawers.

At last my mother went shopping and I quietly made my way to her bedroom. All I found in one drawer was a very small dingy looking leather bound book and the title on it was Aristotle Works. But when I opened it and turned the pages I was quite shocked. The picture that stuck in my mind for many days was of a tummy with three babies curled up inside it. In spite of being unable to understand the book, whenever possible I would continue to look at the pictures and read all about them. In later years the mysteries of life were more easily understood.

For instance to read when so young that a single tiny cell penetrates and fertilises an egg cell and causes it to develop into a new living being was beyond all understanding and I marvelled at the strange power to create bone and muscle, nerves and brain – to bring to that new life those complete details of face, features, complexion and even of mind and character which the parents possessed. When I was old enough to understand the facts of life then I looked back and was grateful for having the chance to read a book of this description.

In the other small drawer was a most peculiar object. One end looked like the rubber hooter of the old fashioned car horns but on the other end attached to the rubber was a glass funnel thing. Being the youngest child I had never seen a baby breast fed and was not to know that this contraption was to remove the mother's milk should she produce too much.

Really I should have been born a boy. For instance my brother Robert arrived home from London on a motor cycle. As he put this machine safely away in the wash house he turned to me and said, "You must not touch my motor cycle or you may get hurt". Oh boy! how exciting. I waited for the moment when the coast was clear and I could explore the parts of this beautiful machine. But alas on climbing on to the seat and jogging up and down on it the bike fell over, taking me with it. My left knee was hurting so much and blood was pouring down my leg. But I dare not go indoors to admit to what I had been up to. I went to the pump in the yard, put some water into the trough and bathed my knee with my handkerchief. To this day I bear the scar of this foolish incident.

The boys always had more interesting hobbies than we girls. Before Robert returned to London he decided he would take out the Landau but with Nobby drawing it instead of Tom. Now Tom was a small pony and was always used solely for this purpose but very slow. Nobby was a big fine horse but kept for farm work and drawing the trap. Robert called to me to go for a ride with him. It was great travelling fast along the country lanes but on the return journey something startled Nobby causing the landau to hit him across his rear. My, how he moved, faster and faster. How we turned two corners as we travelled through the village I do not know. On approaching the farm field gate Robert realised that Nobby was going far too fast to turn in, as much as he tried to rein him in. Robert grabbed me and jumped clear leaving Nobby to go on his way. He just hurtled down towards the river but somehow stopped at the water's edge. Horses are wonderful creatures. It was evident that he could smell the river water and just stopped.

My father came out absolutely furious and shouting his head off. It seems Nobby was too big for the Landau so from the start of the journey Robert and I had a lucky escape. But I loved every bit of it. It was absolutely fantastic flying through the air at great speed.

On one occasion when Edgar came home he brought a box of expanders with him. I would watch, fascinated as he did his exercises. Somehow, I wanted to have a go with them and I wished he would go away for a while. Eventually he set off with our mother and father to go into Horncastle. They wanted me to go along too but I said that I wanted to stay at home. In fact I had those expanders on my mind. I could not stretch them across my chest so I put one on my foot and pulled very hard. Oh dear! it slipped off my foot and hit the ceiling and made the biggest hole. Unfortunately for me the ceilings in the cottage were very low. There was no way out of this but for me to tell the truth when my parents and brother arrived home. No wonder I was sent off to bed immediately.

two
DAVID and ROSE

*D*avid took an active part in the village sports. He organised a football team made up of the local lads. Their opponents came from the other villages. One day one of the boys turned up wearing his mother's navy bloomers as the family were very poor and such things as football shorts were indeed a luxury. David came to his rescue and with money out of the funds a pair of shorts was purchased. During the games a collection would be made and Rose Bell had a stall from which she sold soft drinks, the profit going into the funds. David would also organise whist drives and dances to raise funds for Lincoln Hospital.

Unless the village hall was engaged for other purposes David would be seen teaching the young lads to play billiards. Looking back, snooker was not so popular then.

For years David had grown willow trees, for the making of cricket bats, in the old disused canal which ran through the fields. One wonders if men like Herbert Sutcliffe, Denis Compton and Len Hutton and many others could have played cricket with bats made from the trees grown in Kirkby-on-Bain. Men would come along and measure and mark the trees which were suitable for this particular purpose. They were followed by a team of men who felled them and took them away.

David was a great story teller. The story that intrigued the children most was one of his experiences when he sat with a sick elderly gentleman during the night at a house which was some distance away from the farm. There was a lovely fire burning as he entered the bedroom. The brass fireguard, coal scuttle and fire irons glistened in the glow of the fire. The old gentleman laid quietly in his bed with just his nightcap showing above the bedclothes. David made himself comfortable in his usual armchair and just closed his eyes and relaxed enjoying the fire. After a little time David was aware of a movement of the bedclothes. Still sitting quietly but with one eye partly open he watched the old boy. He got out of bed in his long white flowing night-shirt, looked at David and thought that he was asleep. Then he walked across to the fireplace, picked up the poker and turned towards David. David moved very quickly, firstly grabbing the poker then talking quietly he settled the old man down once more in his bed. Right through the ages children have loved a frightening story even though they feel a little fear.

About two weeks before Christmas David would get up early and fill the copper with water from the pump before making a fire of logs underneath it to heat the water. He would then get out from one of the sheds a strange looking four legged slatted stretcher called a pig cratch. I once saw all this taking place and knew what to expect and just hated the thought of it. Bill Thornley (also the sweep), a tough middle aged fellow, arrived at 8 o'clock with a bag of tools on his back. He and David grabbed hold of the pig by its ears and brought it towards the cratch where it was securely tied and stabbed with a long handled knife. The squealing seemed never ending and reached a high pitch. Then slowly it died down and I realised that the pig was now dead. Hot water was poured over the pig to make the hairs easier to scrape off. Then the cratch with the pig aboard was carried into the kitchen garden, strung up on a high tripod and cut open. Offal's were removed and David would drape the skin with a lacy looking intestine of the pig over the top part of its body which always looked so artistic. Actually he was always very proud of the way it looked as it hung there to cool until about 4 o'clock in the afternoon.

During the day David would carry the salting tub and put it on the floor of the dairy. From time to time one could see the blue tits having a peck at the pig's flesh. Just before dusk David began the process of cutting up the pig. The hams were a lovely sight, David stripped the flitches of their bone structures, and these were eaten as spare ribs which when cooked were delicious. Part of the back of the neck was cut out and along with the hams and flitches and trotters (pig's feet) was carefully laid in the flat tub and covered in common salt for curing. David also used Salt Petre on the bones of the hams to keep the flies at bay.

Meanwhile Rose Bell was very busy. She was very fussy. The best cuts of flesh were put aside for the Pork Pies. Special pastry was used for the pies and the shapes made round a wooden mould. She made tassels of pastry for the tops of the pies, and tiny circles by using a thimble to cut them out which were placed ad lib on the sides. These were glazed with beaten yolks of egg and baked in the oven. When they came out of the oven they looked absolutely delicious.

Next the Haslet was prepared ready for the oven. These were almost the shape of haggis but were encircled with the lacy skin from the stomach of the pig which made them look very professional.

Rose Bell also excelled in making the sausages. The skins or thalms as they were called had previously been soaked in salt water for at least three days then scraped very gently with a spatula to remove any sediment. Out came the sausage machine which was fastened securely to the old pine kitchen table.

Once the sausages were made Rose Bell picked them up in long lengths and tied them up, linking them to the length of the average sausage.

What was left of the meat was made into brawn. Everything from the pig was used, all but its tail. When the hams and flitches and the special cut from the back of the neck called a chine were preserved they were then hung on the wall to dry.

Pig fries were sent to the friends. On each plate was placed a piece of pork, liver and kidney. Once the pig was brought indoors our first meal was the pig's fry. When the parsley in the garden was ready for picking the chine was put on a board and cut into thin slices up to the bone and filled tightly with chopped parsley. It was then tied in a piece of clean linen and boiled until cooked. When cold it was served sprinkled with salt and pepper and vinegar and eaten with a salad, a very tasty dish.

All the fat from the pig was rendered down for lard. Even the scraps from this were very tasty. Actually for weeks they were spoilt for choice. Rose Bell preferred not to use the bladder of the pig in which to store the lard. Instead David used a cycle pump and blew it up and handed it to us to use as a football. When a man is bald one often hears the expression "like a bladder of lard" – this is where it originates.

Rose Bell was a woman of many talents. To care for such a large family must have been very hard work, which included a full day's washing on a Monday. David would fill the copper in the wash house with water and light the fire below

to heat it. When the water was sufficiently hot Rose Bell ladled some of it into a dolly tub, put in soap and the clothes and rotated these by using dolly pegs. All water had to be carried from the pump or rain water butts time and time again until all the clothes were washed. When at last all were clean she would put them through a mangle to squeeze out all the surplus water before pegging them out on the lines.

Ironing seemed to go on for days, fitted in with all the other jobs that had to be done: attending to the milk, making butter, bread and cake making, cooking the meals. She must have been a very strong woman to care for a husband and twelve children and live to the age of 73 years.

At harvest time she made delicious rabbit pies, also home brewed beer for the men bringing home the harvest and for the men when they came into the yard with the threshing machine.

It was lovely to watch the threshing engine and to see the corn separated from the straw. The men doing this expected to be fed too.

Cooking had to be done in the oven, which was part of a Victorian cooking range, with a boiler at the side which had to be kept filled with water at all times, fire in the middle and the oven to the right.

For ironing the irons rested on a grid in front of the fire and when Rose Bell was ironing she removed one of the irons with a cloth holder, spat on the iron to test the heat before rubbing it with a clean cloth to remove any dust from the coal fire.

Milk had to be separated each morning and evening with a special machine called a separator. The milk was poured into the bowl at the top, the motor revved by turning a handle which made the cream come out of one spout and separated milk from the other spout. This milk was usually fed to the pigs.

When sufficient cream was collected it was put into a churn, again turning a handle to revolve the churn until the cream turned to butter. The butter was rinsed in clear water to remove any traces of buttermilk, then made into slabs.

I am indeed a replica of my mother Rose Bell. Like her, I have enjoyed the country life and animals, although with the help of modern appliances which make life easier.

Looking back over the years there was a richness which seems to be missing from the lives of children today. Our parents could not afford expensive presents but somehow we were happier with the simple things of life.

On Winter evenings there were many games to choose from such as Ludo, Snakes and Ladders, Draughts and Dominoes. The only game my parents objected to was the game of Snap. We would get very excited and yell at the top of our voices. Sometimes an argument would arise when someone cheated by looking at their card before turning it over and thus shouting Snap before the others had even looked at theirs. My father would overhear this and then intervene, threatening to send us to bed. Immediately we heard this we promised to be good and were allowed to stay up a little longer.

A quieter game was Hunt the Thimble, or I Spy With My Little Eye something beginning with L and so on. Once one little boy came up with something beginning with S. We thought of everything in the room but to no avail. Consequently we had to give in. You can imagine how we all felt when he said "Ceiling".

We all loved it when it began to snow. After school we would put on our wellingtons, woolly hats and gloves and have the time of our lives snowballing each other. Out would come the sledges, wooden and very home-made, but great fun anyway. The bigger boys would prefer to clear a long stretch of the road and make a slide. Before going indoors we always made a snowman. I would leave the others and sneak into the house to get one of my father's old pipes for the snowman's mouth.

One day as the snow was gradually melting two horsedrawn gypsy caravans came through the village. The little chimneys were smoking away but the village boys had other things on their minds. They hurriedly made hard snowballs out of the melting snow and the next thing I saw was the whole lot of them throwing them at the chimneys almost knocking them off the caravans. Then they took to their heels and ran off to hide behind the very high wall of the Rectory. As they passed me they said "Don't you dare tell the gypsies where we are hiding".

Presently two men from the caravans approached me. I felt very nervous and afraid. In a very gruff voice one man said "Have you seen some boys running along here? We want to catch them." Trembling I quietly said "No" knowing only too well where they could be found.

When I went home I told my mother what I had done. My parents always brought me up not to tell lies and this bothered me. However, my mother reassured me and said, "Never mind, sometimes to prevent someone getting hurt you are allowed to tell what is called a little white lie".

When Spring came with the lighter evenings, out would come the Whips and Tops. There was very little traffic so we had the whole of the road in which to enjoy this sport. Jessie, my friend, was always the winner. There was no one as expert as she.

We would also make squares in the road with chalk and play Hop Scotch. The girls had skipping ropes but the boys joined in when the old clothes line came out and several of them could have a go.

Then there was marbles, faggies if you were lucky enough to have any left from the previous day. Sometimes the boys would try to make their own fireworks. This was nothing new as right through the ages boys have always had to experiment with something or other. Their favourite mixture was Carbide mixed with water. Carbide was used in the old acetylene bicycle lamps. When the Carbide and water was mixed together it was put into bottles and the cork was pushed in tightly. Immediately this was complete the bottles were thrown some distance away. One waited and then suddenly there was a bang as the bottles exploded. On one occasion one bottle failed to explode and Sidney, one of the village lads, went to investigate. As he approached he looked down and the bottle exploded in his face. He was rushed to hospital where he was found to have lost the sight of one eye.

The boys would await the baker's horse drawn van as he went on his rounds and as he drove along one of the lanes they would hang on to a rail at the back of the van and lift up their feet and take rides this way. To me it looked very exciting so one day when no-one was about I grabbed the rail. But alas! the baker did not stop at the next lot of houses so that I could let go, he just kept going. My arms were tired and my legs ached and I had to let go, but not before my knees had trailed on the ground and had got badly cut. I was in great pain and cried and cried. At last I made it to the first little cottage in Wharf Road where lived a lovely old lady we all called Granny Waller. Although she wore a man's cap and smoked a pipe everybody loved her and if in trouble all went to her. As soon as she saw me she put me on her couch and gave me a cup of milk. Then she carefully bathed my knees and put on some ointment and tied a man's handkerchief around each knee. It hurt so terribly as she bathed my knees. When I felt a bit better she took me home and explained what had happened so I escaped the telling off that I had anticipated. Mind you, I was warned not to do such stupid things in the future.

Summertime was usually spent down at the river. Just downstream from the Mill Pool were stepping stones so that you could cross from one side of the river to the other without getting your feet wet. There we would have a whale of a time! That I must say is an amusing expression, maybe a minnow or two but not a whale. With our jam jars to the ready each stone would be carefully lifted. Usually underneath were Stickle-backs but there were at times fish at least three inches long with a big head which we called Bully Heads or Tommy Roughs. Carefully scooping our hands together we would then encircle the fish and grab it. The Bully Heads were more difficult to catch and would take to their fins and quickly swim away.

There were plenty of willow trees from which we cut branches to make fishing rods. Our mothers gave us some thread and the ideal hooks were the pins that held magazines together. For the floats chicken feathers were used. We would use worms or bread soaked in water and squeezed in an old piece of cloth for bait. I must admit we rarely caught anything this way.

For swimming the girls kept their knickers on and the boys their pants if they were lucky enough to have any. Otherwise they just went in with their shorts on and when they reached home just said, "Well I fell in". The boys would go into one of the fields to play football and cricket whilst the girls made daisy chains.

One day I suggested to my mates that we fetched the flat bottomed tub from the shed. This was used once a year as a salting tub to preserve the hams and flitches when the pig was killed. It was a big heavy thing, but eventually we reached the river bank and lowered it into the water. But alas! it just sank. So much for my idea of a boat. It took ages to get it out of the river let alone drag it up the bank. We pushed and shoved to get it back to the shed. Of course my father appeared at the wrong moment and I had a good telling off. My punishment was a whack on the bottom with a special hair brush which he kept for the job, but up to date I had not tasted this.

The highlight of the summer was the harvesting of the corn. My Uncle Arthur and brother-in-law Bill always came from London at this time of year to join in the activities. The day arrived. We children were loaded into their car setting off for the harvest field. It was a very busy time of year on the farm and we were so lucky to be allowed to participate. As we entered the field two men were already cutting down the corn with scythes on the extreme edge, clearing a way for the reaper.

The horses were getting restless and raring to go. Before setting off my father put a large ball of string or what was commonly called twine into a compartment on the reaper binder.

Very soon my father was on his way, we children were fascinated to see the first sheaves falling from this machine already tied up. Both my uncle and brother-in-law were excellent marksmen in the shooting of rabbits as they tried to escape the long knife of the binder.

Once all the corn was layered my father sent two men to collect the basket of food and drink prepared by my mother. We could hardly wait for the food to arrive. In spite of grubby hands we all sat round and tucked into slices of bread and chunks of cheese and pickled onions, followed by scrumptious home-made buns. A large flagon of home-made beer was passed round the men to quench their avid thirst whilst we enjoyed the favourite lemonade made of kali and water. Once all the food was devoured, everyone set to work putting all the sheaves into what were called stooks. It was great fun playing hide and seek amongst these stooks. They made very good hiding places. The game was short lived, suddenly my father called out, "Time to go home". We were not sorry really, everyone was tired, hot and dirty.

My mother took one look at me and very soon had me in the bath tub. It was lovely to feel clean and fresh once more. Then she made me some sandwiches and a small cake and a mug of cocoa. I was happy to go to bed, not before saying my prayers – God bless Mummy, God bless Daddy, Thank you God for a lovely day, God bless me!

When the sheaves were sufficiently dry my father harnessed two horses and put them in the shafts of the big wagon, we all clambered aboard and away to the harvest field to collect the sheaves. We children waited patiently for the last load which was usually much smaller, then we knew we would be thrown up by the strong arms of the menfolk to travel back to the farmyard!

Days later, one heard the sound of the threshing machine coming through the village on its way to the farmyard. On this occasion we were only allowed to stand and watch. We stood in awe once this machine got into action. It did smell a bit oily though. The elevator took up the straw as two men spread it out very methodically to make a stack, whilst my father kept his eye on the grain pouring into great sacks. When each was full he wheeled it in to the barn on a sack barrow. Today threshing machines like this are a prize possession and much sought after by antique collectors.

The following Sunday we children took our gifts of fruit and vegetables when we attended Sunday School. The Chapel had already been adorned with flowers and produce given by our parents. It was a beautiful sight to behold. The apples had lovely shiny red skins, there were huge marrows, pumpkins, tomatoes, cucumbers and pears but the thing that stood out amongst it all was the sheaf of corn made by the baker with dough.

The service in the evening was attended by all the villagers. The hymn "All things bright and beautiful" was sung heartily by everyone.

On the Monday evening the produce was sold in the school room. Can you guess by whom? My father of course. He was a dab hand at the job. Not the usual kind of auctioneering – it had to be a Dutch auction. To us children it sounded a bit Dutch. Instead of the price rising as the bidding went on my father started say at a pound and came down to the price of whatever the goods made. Perhaps they finished up at five shillings or so.

At that time I believe it was law for such auctions to be executed in this way. The proceeds of the auction were sent to Lincoln Hospital along with the flowers.

Once the darker evenings approached and autumn was on its way the game of Hunt the Fox was the first favourite. To choose the fox the method of *dipping* was used as it has been right through the ages. Going from one to the other as we stood in a circle one of us would point and say

> *Eeny Meeny Miny Mo*
> *Catch a rabbit by his toe*
> *If he squeals let him go*
> *Eeny Meeny Miny Mo*

When the fox was chosen, off he would go leaving the rest of us to count to one hundred before taking off to find him. If he found a good hiding place and was hard to find then the followers would call "Sound your hollow and the dogs will follow". Suddenly he would let out a howl but no one ever found him by tracing this noise. Whoever finally found the fox automatically became the next fox.

When we were fed up with this game we had a Paper Chase. This was never very popular. Someone set off maybe across the fields to the woods dropping bits of paper as they went along, leaving a trail for us to follow until they were found. The worst thing about this game was that our parents insisted that we collected the paper afterwards.

Then as it became dark, although we were always dead scared, we all assembled at the outer wired door of the Church to take part in the spooky game of the evening. One of us would tie the much used red and white spotted handkerchief on to the knob of the door. Once this was done we raced round the Church three times but on the last run had to touch the handkerchief and it was so impressed on our minds that at this moment the Devil would appear that we just took to our legs and flew down the main footpath towards the entrance gate and out on to the road. The handkerchief was left tied to the knob as not one of us dared to retrieve it until the next day in daylight.

On November 5th the children would dress up in old clothes, put on a mask bought at the village shop for 2d and set off round the village choosing the houses where they thought their luck would be in. When they knocked on the door the following is what you would hear each child say:

> *Please to remember the 5th of November*
> *The poor old Guy*
> *A piece of bread to stick in his head*
> *A piece of cheese to choke him*
> *A barrel of beer to wash it down*
> *A very good fire to roast him*
> *Hole in my stocking*
> *Hole in my shoe*
> *Please can you spare a copper or two*
> *If you cannot spare a penny, a half-penny will do*
> *If you cannot spare a half-penny then God bless you*

Very few of our parents failed to make a contribution.

three
PRIMARY SCHOOL

$\mathcal{T}$he entrance to the Church of England Primary school was from the narrow School Lane through a very big door into what was actually the older boys cloak room. From the cloak room a large oak door opened into the main class room. Half way down another door opened into the infants' room and right at the end was another door leading into the girls and infants' cloak room. From this cloak room were two more doors, one leading into the infants' room and the other to the outside door to the girls toilet. The toilet was the old double decker closet, the taller seat for the bigger girls and the little one for the tiny tots. The boys could only approach their toilet by going out of the main door, a little way down the school lane opposite the entrance to the playground. The double decker closet was the same but the boys also had a trough.

In the cloak rooms were the old free-standing stands with the enamel wash bowls inside and an enamel jug underneath for water. The soap was really horrible and the towels too hard to dry one's hands on.

The lovely old striking village clock had a prominent position on the outside of one of the main walls, with the works encased in lovely polished wood on the inside of the main classroom.

As the time approached for me to attend school, my mother spoke with the Head Mistress to arrange for me to start school in September, my fifth birthday being in October. Otherwise I would have had to wait until the following January. My first day at school was a most memorable day in my life. Would you believe it, I bit one of the boys and when I meet this boy, now a man in his seventies, he still reminds me of this incident. Neither of us can remember why I bit him but I no doubt had my reasons or perhaps even at this age I wanted to prove I was a force to be reckoned with.

Some of my friends were a year or two older so they soon helped me to adjust. What's more the infant teacher was well known in the village, being the daughter of the shopkeeper.

The school bell would be tolled by the Head Mistress herself at 8.40 each morning calling all the children to school. This was the first warning, but by

8.55 we had to stand in a line in the main porch before entering the main school room. The Head Mistress, Miss Frances Logan (nick-named Totty) called out the register, then proceeded towards the old harmonium and commenced playing. She looked so odd rocking from side to side as she pedalled away. We dare not look at each other in case we laughed. After the hymn, prayers were said, and the infants were then marched into the little classroom at the side of the main hall. For our first lesson a sand tray full of lovely silver sand was put in front of each child. The teacher would write a letter on the black board which we learned to copy by making signs in the sand. This was such a lovely way to teach us, the sand being so nice to the touch of one's finger. The method was called Montessori. Although a splendid way in which to teach young children it would be too expensive in this day and age. Learning the alphabet this way seemed so much easier to grasp.

Counters were used to teach us to add up. The balls frame, or abacus as they are commonly known, were a great favourite.

In one corner of the room stood a very large sand tray in which the children depicted a different subject every Monday morning. For instance for Christmas there was a typical snow scene. We all took cotton wool for snow and sprigs of fir trees but the teacher always made the snowman and Santa Claus. We had great fun cutting out boats and using match stalks for the masts for the scene of the sea. Then there was the farmyard. Some of the children brought toy animals from home. For each scene the teacher would encourage us to tell her in detail what we knew about each subject.

Reading was more difficult. Over the years the memories of the cards with cat, dog, etc. still remain. Pointing with my first finger I can recall, "Rover is my dog".

On a warm summer's day the teacher would take us down the country lanes on a nature walk. We all loved this, stopping on our way to watch the bees entering the flowers, counting how many butterflies we had seen. Most of all we loved to watch the beautiful birds as they flitted from tree to tree.

The things we most disliked were the slates and slate pencils, as they screeched when writing.

When Friday came along the teacher would ask us to take any kind of empty box, tin or packet which our mothers had discarded. These were assembled on a table and prices written on them and we had to pretend we were going shopping. Someone was chosen for the shopkeeper. We were each given cardboard coins and the teacher would stand by to watch and correct any mistakes that were made in paying for the purchase.

About half an hour before the end of the school day we all sat round and the teacher would read a lovely story to us.

They were such happy days but to be short lived once we moved into the big classroom. My brother George hated school to the extent that Father had to drag him to school every day and push him through the door so that he could not escape.

The older children always appeared afraid of Miss Logan. No wonder. She was so unkind and used the cane relentlessly on each child even if they made only a small mistake in their work. Eventually the time came when I had to move into this class. I was very tense and nervous and wondered what would happen to me.

Over the main entrance door hung a large picture of Edith Cavell. From time to time I would glance up at her and wish that one day I too could become a nurse. To me her picture was a great inspiration. Sadly over the years it has been removed. Changes take place and not always to improve the way of life. She should be remembered for her great work which eventually cost her her life on October 12th 1915.

She was a matron in a hospital in Brussels and was shot by the Germans for helping Allied troops to escape into Holland. Eventually she was buried in Norwich Cathedral. Her last recorded words were, "I realise patriotism is not enough".

Every Friday afternoon two children were selected to collect the ink-wells, to empty and wash them out and to leave them to drain over the weekend. On Monday morning new ink was prepared in powder form, mixed with water, and the ink-wells were replenished for the forthcoming week. Sometimes we had to use slates and slate pencils. The slate had a frame of wood encircling it to prevent us being cut by the sharp edges, the pencil was of very fine slate. Oh! the screechy noise they made was at times unbearable, it would "set my teeth on edge".

Totty should never have been a teacher. Previously she had been a governess to the children of a very rich family.

At times she would be seen going along the hedgerows choosing a branch for a cane. On my first caning I told her that I would tell my mother. She gave me another wack across the palm of my hand and said, "Now go and tell your mother". We were not naughty or lazy children, just solely caned for giving a wrong answer.

During the Summer holidays she would go to America on the ship the Mauritania of the Cunard Star Line and oh! how we wished this ship would sink while she was on it.

One day one of the boys was so fed up with receiving so many blows with the cane that he picked up the scuttle of coke which was always ready to stoke the old combustion stove and threw it all over her. She was absolutely livid and just madly caned and caned him.

One poor lad had to remove his trousers to take his punishment on his bottom. He was so embarrassed as he was not wearing any underpants. She instructed him to lie face downwards on the desk and began to hit him. As he wriggled his little whistle nearly went into the ink well.

When one stood next to her one could smell cigarettes and wine. Our parents could be heard discussing the delivery of wines and cigarettes from a very big firm in London. Perhaps we suffered when she had been drinking. In fact she may have been a very sick woman who was in need of treatment. Eventually she went too far with her caning. A girl called Joyce was caned so much that her thumb on her left hand was like a piece of black jelly. Her parents threatened to take Miss Logan to court but at the request of the Governors she was asked to resign.

We all breathed a sigh of relief.

Kirkby-on-Bain primary school, c.1926. Dorothy Rose, aged about 9, is on the front row, third girl from the right.

In 1930 a new head mistress was appointed by the name of Miss Weale. She was a lovely person and so kind. Sadly though she only stayed for a year. It would appear that at weekends she was supposed to be visited by an uncle. Day by day we noticed that she was putting on weight. Naturally we heard whispers from our elders and became aware that she was expecting a baby. One day she appeared to be in great pain and had to leave the class room. Sadly we never saw her again. To replace Miss Weale another teacher was appointed. Her name was Mrs Florence Watkin, a widow. She was very stern but also very kind and thoughtful. It seemed our caning days were over. What fascinated us was that when she got out of her chair she would throw back and straighten her shoulders very military-like but at the same time emphasising her ample bosoms and making her nipples become very prominent under her fine silk light brown dress. At sewing time we girls were very amused. We would rush to get the thimbles and push them under our blouses or jumpers to be Mrs Watkin look-alikes.

Under Mrs Watkin's supervision we learned far more and enjoyed school. When out in the playground one day we looked through the slits in the very high fence towards some old stables where a man called Ernest Adams kept his mare. As we watched, another horse came along the road, a huge horse bedecked with beautiful brasses and ribbons, led into the stables by a man who was carrying a little bag on the end of a long stick which rested on one shoulder just like Dick Whittington. We all gazed intently as these two horses pranced around in the yard. Being so young we were not aware of what it was all about. In later years when we heard the usual story of the birds and the bees then the answer was quite simple. Eventually Mrs Watkin realised what was happening and called us inside. Throughout early spring these men would walk many miles from village to village offering the services of their very beautiful stallions.

On days that were not spent at school I would wander off sometimes over the bridge to the fields beyond. One particular day this was very lucky for Nobby, the horse used for the trap, as he was knee deep in the mud in the canal and try as hard as he could he could not get out. I ran home and told Father whereupon he called for help with more horses to pull Nobby out. There were no tractors at that time and it took three big horses to drag him out of the mud. He looked a right mess and had to have a scrub down.

As far back as I can remember I have always loved flowers. I would pick sweet smelling violets from the hedgerow and primroses from the wood. There was a disused lock adjoining the canal. Looking down into it I spotted some beautiful yellow water lilies. I just could not resist these. It was a long way down and in places water was trickling out of the brickwork. Long grasses were growing at the sides too. So I gently lowered myself, hanging on to these grasses as I went down on to the very narrow ledge at the side of the lock. I reached out and picked some lilies. But it was not until I looked up that I was aware of the danger I was in. How was I to get out? Getting down was easy. I had my lovely lilies and just had to get out. Stuffing the lilies securely under my jumper I tried the way I came down. The grasses were still tight into the grooves of the wall. It seemed such a long way to the top but I made it. It was when I looked down again from the top that I really began to be afraid. I could have slipped into the green slimy water and drowned and may never have been found. I never told anyone the story of the lock until years later.

My name still remains in the School Record Book even to the present day. It says that on 29th October 1930 Rose Cook picked up a cricket bat with which to play Rounders. A boy named Raymond Butler stood right behind her as she raised and swung the bat to hit the ball and she hit him. He immediately fell flat on his back and lay quite still. He was rushed to hospital and to my relief was back at school the next day.

When I was eleven years old I should have taken the 11 Plus Exam. The Headmistress was very concerned as I was most unsettled so she talked to my parents. They explained the reason for my not wishing to get on with my work. She then advised my parents that in my interest it was unwise to take this exam.

My sister Violet who was just eighteen years old had been ill for over a year and had just died. This was a great shock to me. I used to sit with her so much and when she was no longer there I missed her terribly. It was all so sad. She looked so beautiful with her coppery coloured hair and smooth complexion, yet suffered greatly. The pain was often so intense she would cry out. But under the bedclothes one saw just a body of skin and bone. Even between her knees was a little down cushion to prevent them rubbing together causing more pain. I was in no fit state to sit for any exam watching all this suffering to such a lovely girl. Years previously my father had planted a Cox's Orange Pippin apple tree and this was always known as Violets' tree. Strange as it may seem the tree seemed to die too. Yet at the time when I was getting married this tree came back to life. Strange things happen between heaven and earth about which we have no understanding.

Later on I felt robbed of the chance of further education. If I had passed then I would have gone to the Grammar School at Horncastle. But my father always maintained that each one of his children after leaving school should get a job and support themselves. So even if I had passed with flying colours he would have stood in the way of further education.

Therefore the footpath of life led on in a different direction.....

When I was just twelve years old Miss Joachim, the headmistress of the Girls' High School, asked me to take part in a Pageant that she was organising in the Winter Gardens to raise money for the Alexandra Hospital. The Winter Gardens was a beautiful building with a very large stage, attractive alcoves and a balcony on three sides of the hall. Sadly it was destroyed when two parachute mines were dropped on Woodhall Spa on 23rd August 1942.

Miss Joachim could have chosen any one of her girls for the part which I was to play, and over the years I have wondered why she chose me. My brother Arthur serviced her car and I had been at the garage on several occasions when she came along. It could not have been to please my brother. If she had been twenty years younger then one might have thought she fancied him and was using me to gain his affection.

Anyway my part in the Pageant seems very vague after all these years. I remember being a Bride, beautifully attired in a beaded and embroidered dress and veil. As I walked on to the stage there sat the Bridegroom's father with the Bride's father at a table thoroughly enjoying a sumptuous meal. I don't even remember seeing the Bridegroom.

Because of the livestock, Rose Bell and David always went their separate ways for their holidays. Rose Bell would take me to London on the train to stay with my sister Lily and her husband. David would go with a barber friend from Horncastle to the Ascot Races. Out would come the Gladstone Bag and his posh brown boots with their beige cloth tops which looked like spats. The holiday I remember best was in October 1930 when I saw the Air Ship R1001 going over London before it crashed in France.

My brother George would get out his bicycle and, with his pals ride into Horncastle to have a game of billiards. One night in June 1931, as he walked into the dairy to get his supper, the pots on the shelf began to rattle. David and Rose Bell were awakened by the unusual noise going on downstairs, and so was I. Naturally as this noise occurred soon after George had entered the house David was convinced George was to blame. I listened intently, wondering what David would find. The next thing we heard was David bellowing out "What the bloody hell are you up to?" George was amazed and so were we when George explained about the crockery and the saucepans in the pantry. It was not until the next day that we were told that it had been an earth tremor.

It was a very sad day when Tom the pony became too old to draw the open Landau. I overheard my mother and father discussing having him put down and that my father had arranged for a man to do this down by the river. I watched my father cross the river to the fields beyond and put a halter around Tom's neck. Then he walked him down to the shallow part of the water's edge where stood this man with a gun in his hand. There was a bang and Tom fell to the ground. I was absolutely stunned and almost collapsed with shock. Then I ran home and into my bedroom and laid on the bed just sobbing away. For days my parents were very quiet. They too must have been terribly upset. My father then sold the old Landau and bought an old car, the back of which was altered to take chicken crates.

Nobby was a very fine horse, big and strong and would pull the trap with very little effort. Before my father purchased him he had hunted with the hounds. Consequently as my father was ploughing one day in the distance could be heard the huntsman's horn and away went Nobby dragging both the plough and my father along with him. After this my father made sure of the days when the hunt would be in that area. As I write this the memories return. It is as if I almost hear the sound of the wheels of the trap and of Nobby high stepping as my father came down the lane after a day at the market in Boston. Knowing he was nearing home Nobby seemed to gallop even faster down the lane. On entering the field gate my father would take Nobby out of the shafts and loosen his harness. But until my father whistled Nobby would not attempt to urinate.

The Rector and his wife were such lovely people. They had the welfare of the villagers at heart. On Easter Sunday they would hide Easter Eggs in the grounds of the Rectory and invite the children to go and hunt for them. From a young age I was always interested in nature. Even though one was carefully looking for an egg I remember so well the huge Copper Beech tree in the centre of the lawn with this gorgeous carpet of purple, purple and white, yellow and white crocuses underneath. The crows and the rooks were kicking up such a din in the trees in the spinney.

On May Day we danced around the Maypole on the main lawn in front of the drawing room windows from which we emerged to take our positions at the Maypole.

When we were about twelve years old we were allowed to play tennis on the court just beyond the ha-ha. The Rector's wife made lovely marmalade and sold this quite cheaply to the members of the Women's Guild. One area of the kitchen garden was totally covered in netting to protect the raspberries and strawberries. Everyone had the privilege to pick whatever fruit they desired. Then you reported to the Rectory kitchen to have it weighed and pay for it.

Although it was a small community there was always something to occupy one's time. Once the Lilies of the Valley were coming in to bloom we set off to the woods belonging to the Hawley family at Tumby, a little hamlet a short distance from the village. On one occasion I went on my bicycle with one of the girls Eva to pick some lilies but it was not long before I came to grief. I slammed my brakes on too fast to turn into a gateway at the entrance to the woods and just flew over the handlebars, landing on a most uneven gravel cart track. I finished up with severe gravel rash on one elbow and had to go to the doctor. To this day I have a scar on my left elbow in the shape of a butterfly. Once I recovered from my wounds Eva and I set off again to gather the much loved Lilies-of-the-Valley. We were both happily picking away, walking further and further into the woods unaware of the hour of the night. Gradually darkness overtook us and whichever way we walked we could not find a gap in the ferns and trees to indicate we were at the edge of the wood. Eventually we both sat down and cried. We were real life Babes in the Wood. Thinking of creepy crawlies and snakes and having to stay there all night urged us to try again to get out into the open. First we tried one path made by the gamekeeper, then another. We were so afraid, when suddenly a clearing appeared before us and at last we were safe.

This was my last visit to these woods, after having learnt another lesson. It is quite true that you live and learn – not always the easy way. On leaving school, when I was fifteen years old, I was appointed by the Vicar and the school Governors to become the teacher to the infants and I held this post for two years.

Having been taught in this school made it easier for me to teach the children in a similar way. In those days it was unnecessary for a certificated teacher to fill this post. The only difference was that the inner door to the classroom had to be left open at all times for the Headmistress to see how I was progressing. My work with the children apparently pleased both the Headmistress and the parents of the children. On one occasion the School Inspector, Mr Scatterly, complimented me on my work and suggested I spoke with my father to allow me to go on to the Teacher Training College at Lincoln. This sadly was totally out of the question. David insisted that we all made our own way in life.

The Fancy Dress Ball was held annually in the Village Hall and the judge was usually a renowned lady from the next village. As it was nearing November 11th and Remembrance Day I decided to make a Flanders Poppy out of crepe paper. This took much time and patience. I made a pair of green trousers out of material for the stem. The centre was cut out of cardboard and covered with black satin with Earl Haig's Fund printed on it with white chalk, using horse hair from the horses tail for the stamens then circling this with loads of red crepe paper making a very beautiful poppy. On the evening of the parade I carried this flower in front of me.

Mother went as a fortune teller, looking the part with her long black hair. Normally this would be in a bun on top of her head or circles of hair over each ear. Instead she wore it falling down on to her shoulders. To complete the outfit she carried a green glass buoy which looked like her crystal ball.

Now Father had us all guessing, telling us that he had already prepared his fancy dress. Mother and I were both somewhat bewildered and when the parade started who could be seen coming through the hall door but father. What we saw gave us quite a shock. There he was bare body to the waist, his riding breeches on and highly polished leggings just carrying a horse's brush and curry comb.

Lo! and behold he took first prize in the Men's Parade. He told us afterwards he was confident that he would take a prize as he knew the judge was a great horse lover and very keen on joining the local hunt. The lady's prize went to a Victorian lady. Such an easy costume to borrow, I felt a little peeved at my effort being in vain.

During the Summer months the Rector and his wife took in students to swell their income. The stipends in those days were so small that the old adage, "As poor as a Church mouse" fitted the bill. One year two Indian Princes arrived in a beautiful red sports car. They were aged around eighteen, Lech the Chinese Prince seemed a little older. He preferred to borrow a horse to go riding. There were also English students. Fortunately for the villagers they all played musical instruments so every Saturday night instead of dancing to the music of the gramophone they set up a band and played for the dancing.It was very sad when they all departed at the end of the Summer to return to their normal studies.

Once a year the Rector's wife would put on a Concert and most of the young people were happy to participate. On one occasion I was in the play called *Mrs Jarley's Wax Works* as a Fairy. It was very difficult to dance and be a waxwork at the same time. After the rehearsals two people were chosen to clear up the hall in readiness for the snooker in the evening. It just happened that Patrick the Rector's son and I were chosen. After the others had left the hall Patrick just grabbed and kissed me. I was shocked, bewildered and somewhat afraid. After all I was just seventeen years old and had never been kissed before other than by relatives and friends. Once the initial shock was over we sat and talked. Oh yes! he said that I was lovely and that he loved me and would I meet him again?

Our meeting was in the spinney adjoining the Rectory grounds. As I was a great lover of flowers my parents accepted the fact when I informed them that I was going to pick some violets and primroses. Oh! yes I made sure that I had a bunch of each to take home with me.

These meetings were more like the fairy tales I had read in books. It was only natural that I liked to be kissed and cuddled. Sometimes we would meet in Reddings Wood just a little way out of the village. I would cross the fields but Patrick would go by the main road.

The very essence of the surroundings of the wood made our meetings more romantic. The song of the birds filled the air and up in the tall trees the pigeons were cooing to each other. As we walked hand in hand towards our favourite tree trunk we were surrounded by the sweet scent of the violets, the bees were buzzing away amongst the Primroses, Wood Anemones, Lords and Ladies and Celandines. The rabbits scurried away when they heard the crunching of dead branches under our feet. Suddenly a cock pheasant let out his call and flew into a tree. He looked so resplendent with his glossy emerald crown and bright red wattle, his body plumage copper coloured with deep chestnut brown markings and whitish crescents, his tail richly barred, fringed with tints of violet. A splendid sight for us to behold. All this made our meetings more romantic and very precious to us.

These were really brief meetings. We dare not be away too long to give our parents reason to wonder where we had been. Our secret was so very special to the two of us.

One day Patrick went shopping to Lincoln with his mother. How lovely of him, he bought me a bottle of Jasmine perfume. As he was studying Theology at Cambridge he was dependant on an allowance from his parents. I wonder how he managed to sneak away from his mother whilst he purchased the perfume. Oh! boy what would she have said had she been aware of this?

The meeting I shall never forget was my visit to the Rectory. Patrick had sent me a note via the maid, who was sworn to secrecy, asking me to go that evening to the Rectory whilst his parents spent the evening at the Kinema in the Woods at Woodhall Spa. I was very nervous as I walked up the long drive to the front door. I rang the bell and the maid showed me into a beautiful hall with a flagged floor and huge red Turkish rug. Patrick appeared and showed me into the drawing room but not before ordering the maid to bring in two glasses of sherry. What a beautiful room. The colour scheme was a pretty blue. In one corner stood a grand piano, beautiful plates were around the room and an embroidered screen at the door caught my eye. We sat and talked and drank the sherry, then Patrick rang the bell for the maid and asked her to make sure she washed the glasses and put them away. But I was on tenterhooks all the time. Let's face it his parents could have arrived home at any time, and they may not have liked the picture. It was not long before I took my leave.

At least once a year his mother would take us on an outing and hire a bus. Patrick and I sat next to each other on the bus on our journey to Louth. On our way home we called at Somersby, Lord Tennyson's birth place. Patrick's elder

brother was married to the daughter of the owners of the Rectory at that time. Consequently we were all made very welcome and were shown into the bedroom where Lord Tennyson was born. As we walked up the very wide stairs

Somersby Rectory

Patrick whispered in my ear that "we shall have a better house than this". Yet I was enjoying every minute of it after living in a cottage. We were also allowed into the little private Chapel.

After visits of this nature the Rector's wife liked one of us to write an essay. In this instance she requested me to do so. Meanwhile Patrick and I continued to meet. Then one day his mother sent the maid and asked me to go the next afternoon to take the essay if it was finished. I went gaily along unaware of what was awaiting me, thinking all would be accepted if Patrick told his mother that he was in love with me.....

But Oh dear! No. I rang the front door bell and the maid opened the door and showed me into the dining room where stood Patrick's mother. She wasted no time in telling me that we were both too young, that the meetings had to stop and that Patrick had to continue with his studies. It was obvious that Patrick was aware of our conversation. He would play a few notes on the piano, then frantically run up and down the oak polished stairs. Eventually she allowed us to meet for a few minutes to say goodbye and so that was the end of my first romance.

Naturally I was very sad for some time. I told my mother because I knew she would understand. But my father was never told as there would have been quite a scene and I wanted to spare my mother any unhappiness.

Some years later I met Patrick who said to me "I cannot marry you myself but perhaps one day you will allow me to marry you to another man". Unfortunately his family moved away and I never saw him again. The only news I ever had of him was that he had married a nurse. Maybe I would have made a good Vicar's wife.

Most fishermen are noted for telling a story (not always the truth) about the size and weight of their catches. My father was very keen on fishing but rarely caught anything. But when my brother Arthur came home for a few days he would just throw in his line and would have either a chub, a perch or even a trout on the hook. We never understood this. It was almost as if he had hypnotised it.

However there was a very large enemy in the river, a pike, who was enjoying the tasty meals of trout. My father tried all ways of catching this pike even to getting his gun out and taking a shot at him, but to no avail. Then one day he had a clever idea. He made a snare which he carefully placed in the river at the end of a long branch about 2 feet away from the pike. When he gave me a signal then I was to throw in a brick just behind the pike. The pike, startled, made a dash and entered the snare and in seconds he was on the river bank.

When the river was very low then there would be little islands and deep pools. When this occurred my father would teach me to tickle the trout and catch them easily. This I believe is illegal but it happens anyway.

The biggest trout I have ever seen was set up in a glass case. It was caught by Sir David Hawley of Tumby in the River Bain and weighed 4 lbs 6 ozs. My father bought this at an auction sale of the Hawley family. It was in our family for years. When I came to Leicester to live after the Second World War my father gave this trout to me. The glass case required a slight repair and went up to the works to be done. But would you believe it? My sister in law without asking to whom it belonged went off with it to sell at one of her charities. I would have liked to have known who the purchaser was and to know it had a good home.

From time to time I would help my father to put the eel pots or eel baskets into the river. The baskets were long and narrow, wide at the mouth and tapering away to nothing. One thing I would not do was remove these pots from the river and take out the eels. They were too much like snakes. Although very nutritious I could not bear to eat any when they were cooked.

Until my romance with Patrick, thoughts of boy-friends had never entered my head. Then one day one of the village boys who was serving in the Air Force came home on leave. I happened to go into the shop owned by his mother and when I came out he was waiting to speak to me. We stood and talked for a while and before I went on my journey he asked me if I would write to him while he was away as at times he felt very lonely.

In fact I think he must have told his mother that we were pen friends as she appeared extra nice towards me. Just before Percy was due to come on leave he wrote rather an unusual letter to me. In it he stated that he had something of importance to ask me but on no account was I to mention any of this to my parents. This letter to me sounded quite ominous. I could only think of one thing that he would be asking me. In no uncertain words I wrote and told him that if I was right in thinking what he may be asking of me then the answer was definitely NO.

What else could it be. We had not really known each other long enough for him to ask me to wait for him or to become engaged. And anyway if this had been the case then there was no reason whatsoever to be so secretive with regard to my parents. To have any affair with any man was quite out of the question.

I may have misjudged him, that I shall never know. Eventually when he came home on leave he never spoke to me again. I must say whenever we met he always looked somewhat embarrassed. I think of him at times when aircraft fly overhead. He died some years ago and so I say to myself, "Dear Percy, if you are looking down on me from up there, please forgive me if I misjudged you". During the Second World War he piloted Blenheim Bombers.

In fact his mother had a bungalow built and named it Blenheim. Her grandson is now living in the bungalow and it still retains its name.

Dorothy Rose, with Blaze

Any thoughts about Percy were quickly dispelled by the events of the next few days when we heard of the sudden death of Arthur Major. Seeing endless cars and strangers streaming into the village we all realised that something was sadly wrong. There is always gossip in a village and soon the rumours were flying around that there was something sinister about this man's sudden death.

The story began with little Ethel Lillie Brown who was the only girl in a family of four children. She was born on August 6th 1891 at a place called Muckton Bottom about 12 miles from Louth in Lincolnshire. Her father Tom became a gamekeeper on the estate of Sir Henry Hawley who resided with his family in a very grand house in a little hamlet called Tumby just a few miles from the village of Kirkby-on-Bain.

After the family moved to Tumby little Ethel attended a private school at Coningsby until she was old enough to cycle each day to a Council School at Marehem-le-Fen. Her parents were very humble, they made very few friends outside the family circle.

For a young girl there was very little in the way of entertainment to relieve the monotony. She had little choice but to help her mother with the daily chores of the cottage. When she left school her parents had hopes of her being a dressmaker so she was apprenticed to a tailor, but this soon came to an end as her mother's health began to deteriorate and Ethel had no choice but to take over the running of the home.

In her early twenties she became pregnant and gave birth to a daughter in 1915 yet she absolutely refused to disclose the name of the father of this child, though the villagers felt it was likely to be one of the village lads.

In those days there was always stigma as well as gossip attached to an illegitimate child so Ethel's parents decided to pass off this little girl as their own and so she became known as Auriol Iris Tryphone Brown.

When Ethel was 21 years old she met Arthur Major again who in previous years had worked locally as a butcher's boy. On his leaves from the war in France they met frequently and eventually married in June 1918, he to return to the Forces and she to remain with her parents.

Once Ethel was married to Arthur, she and her parents decided that they would not tell Arthur that in fact Auriol was Ethel's daughter and not her sister as everyone was led to believe. In the following May Ethel gave birth to a son whom they christened Lawrence. Somehow, for no reason at all, Arthur showed no affection whatsoever for his son. This, of course, caused friction between the couple. Meanwhile the deception continued as to the truth of Auriol's birth. Eventually all this became a strain on Ethel's mother's health and it was not long before she passed away.

After a while Ethel's father Tom decided to take Auriol with him to live in a little cottage in Roughton, another pretty little village at the foot of the Lincolnshire Wolds, so Ethel, Arthur and Lawrence moved to a bungalow which they rented opposite the Primitive Chapel in the village of Kirkby-on-Bain.

Ethel kept the home spotlessly clean, their living room always looking inviting with its white painted cane chairs. Later on a Council House with a lovely view of the Spinney belonging to the Old Rectory became vacant and they moved there.

Soon there were problems over money, Arthur accusing Ethel of spending more money than they could afford. But worse was to come. Someone told Arthur the truth of Auriol's birth. Naturally when he arrived home to tackle his Ethel over this she had no choice but to admit to her youthful indiscretion and that Auriol was really her daughter and not her sister. They argued because Ethel refused to tell Arthur the name of the man who was Auriol's father. Arthur became very frustrated and angry and from here onwards the marriage began to crumble.

Bitterness set in and Arthur began to drink heavily also seeking solace in the arms of another woman. At this stage Ethel decided to take out a separation and maintenance order against Arthur but eventually he promised to mend his ways so she withdrew her threat.

However, by the Spring of 1934 the marriage was on the rocks. Ethel and Lawrence spent more and more time with her father, still a gamekeeper at Roughton, leaving Arthur to fend for himself. Once again he started drinking heavily yet in spite of this he managed to keep up his job as a lorry driver at the local gravel pits.

Then one day Ethel returned to the council house and found two love letters from Arthur's new found lover. No one knows what passed through her mind at this stage. She must have felt much hatred for him and so the bitterness within her caused her to seek her revenge, and she had a positive plan in her mind.

On Tuesday May 22nd Arthur appeared to be in the best of health. However, as he and the men with whom he worked sat eating their sandwiches he was heard to say, "I reckon my old woman is doing it across me".

On that fateful night he prepared his own meal of corned beef. That evening Lawrence his son arrived home to see his father holding his head in his hands as if he was suffering from a severe headache. Arthur got up out of his chair and went out into the yard, intending to repair his bicycle. But suddenly Lawrence saw his father stagger and slump against a shed obviously in great pain. Lawrence called his mother and together they carried Arthur upstairs and put him to bed. When Tom Brown called that evening he was shocked to see his son-in-law frothing at the mouth and his body wracked with convulsions. Tom could not understand why Ethel had not sent for the doctor, so he decided to do so. Of course, Ethel blamed the corned beef but the doctor, who was new to the area, was convinced he was suffering from epilepsy. Before the doctor left the house he administered both a sedative and medicine to Arthur.

The following day he appeared to be much better. His wife nursed him devotedly bringing lots of cups of tea up to him.

That evening the convulsions returned but again by the morning the condition had improved. About 10 o'clock that third evening he had a relapse and said aloud, "I am going to die". Less than an hour later he died in excruciating pain watched helplessly by his wife and son who still failed to call the doctor.

Ethel worked swiftly and by midnight she had called in the undertakers and insisted that she wanted him buried without delay. Her eagerness to get the funeral over quickly was really the first hint that something was amiss. To cover up the tracks she set off early the next morning to the doctor's surgery, announced the death of her husband. The doctor signed a death certificate giving the cause of death as STATUS EPILEPTEUS.

It was evident that the doctor was not in the least suspicious, having previously visited the home, and arrived at the diagnosis of a sudden fatal epileptic fit. Somewhere, someone knew differently. An anonymous letter was received by the local coroner on the Saturday morning drawing attention to the suspicious death of a dog at a house next door to the Major family. After all these years the identity of this informer has never been revealed.

The residents of this tiny village were absolutely stunned at the sudden death of Arthur Major. Meanwhile Ethel was eager for the funeral to take place on the Saturday, but Arthur's brothers intervened and insisted that it was most disrespectful to proceed so soon after his death, after all he had only passed away on the Thursday night. So really she had no choice but to wait anxiously until the next day.

At 1 o'clock in the afternoon of Sunday May 27th 1934 the family assembled at the house in readiness for the funeral at 3 o'clock. The mourners included Arthur's two brothers, his father-in-law Tom Brown, his fifteen year old son Lawrence and the 19 year old step daughter Auriol.

Suddenly the front door bell rang. Ethel darted nervously into the hall and peeped through the net curtains before answering the door. Her heart fell as she recognised the uniform of the police. An inspector and a constable entered the hall and informed Ethel Major that the funeral would have to be postponed. They said that she was not under suspicion but it was strange that her husband had died so suddenly. After the police left the house Ethel went into the living room and informed the family of the conversation that had taken place between herself and the police.

Even Ethel's father Tom had been somewhat puzzled about the events of the last few days as his son-in-law, who was only 44 years old and was fit and healthy, yet within two days he had become ill and died.

Police enquiries quickly followed and it was established that on the morning of Wednesday 23rd May (after her husband had been taken ill) Ethel Major appeared in the back garden carrying a plate, and scraped the bits on to the ground, whereupon the dog from next door immediately ate up the scraps. That evening the dog was found in obvious pain,. The poor thing was unable to open its mouth but lay rigid with occasional spasms of convulsions. By the next morning the dog was dead.

During the afternoon of Saturday an Inspector Dodson called on the neighbour and they discussed the dog's death. The two men took shovels and dug up the dog from the garden. Then on the Sunday morning the Coroner issued an order halting Arthur Major's funeral and ordered a post-mortem examination on both the dead man and the dog.

Consequently Arthur Major remained unburied whilst organs from his body and those of the dog were minutely scrutinised. Naturally the news leaked out of the events of the past few days and it caused quite a sensation amongst the small community, news which eventually reached the National Press. The village had never before experienced such comings and goings with so many cars in the vicinity. Dr Gerald Roche Lynch, the celebrated Home Office

Analyst, conducted the tests in his laboratory at St. Mary's Hospital, Paddington, West London. He found Strychnine in every organ he examined. It would appear that the first dose was administered on Tuesday 22nd May but as a result of this Arthur did not die. There was no doubt that on the Thursday May 24th he received another dose which actually caused his death. There was also strychnine in the body of the dog.

By July the case was taken up by Scotland Yard and from then onwards the villagers became very aware tof the seriousness of the situation. The sad thing about the whole affair was that the son Lawrence and the father of Ethel Major were subsequently interviewed by the officers from Scotland Yard. Tom Brown agreed that his daughter knew that, as a game keeper, he kept poison in his cottage at Roughton, and that it was kept locked in a box in his bedroom. Also there were two keys to this box but one had gone missing.

On Monday July 9th Inspector Young and his men knocked on the door of Ethel Major's home and when she opened it he announced that he was there to arrest her for Murder. On being questioned by Inspector Young, Ethel Major admitted that she was aware her father kept poison in the house but claimed she did not know where he kept it, nor the key. But her next remark was her downfall as she immediately stated that she did not know her husband had died from the effects of strychnine poisoning. Whereupon Inspector Young asked her how she knew it had been strychnine poisoning to which she replied, "Oh, I must have made a mistake, I did not know what you said." All along Ethel Major protested her innocence. The officers from the Yard searched the house and found a key in a purse which Ethel declared she never used. When they questioned Tom Brown about this key he confirmed that it was the one that had gone missing. To make sure it really was the other key Inspector Young inserted it in the keyhole of the box and it worked perfectly.

Ethel Major's trial took place at Lincoln Assizes where she was found guilty of murder and was hanged at Hull Prison on December 19th 1934. The inhabitants of Kirkby-on-Bain were absolutely shocked at the final outcome.

Young and old alike prayed for the elderly father and her daughter Auriol and her young son Lawrence to give them strength in their grief. No one knows of the anguish, the sorrow and the grief that this family felt on that fateful day.

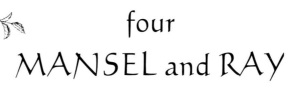

four
MANSEL and RAY

*M*y father was a staunch Liberal and at election time worked very hard for the cause. He and my mother were invited to attend a Whist Drive and Dance in a village called Mareham-le-Fen in aid of funds for the Liberals. My mother was asked to present the prizes, but as she won first prize at Whist the Committee asked me to do the honours.

Once the Whist Drive was over the room was cleared for the dancing. My sister Lily was staying with us at the time and as we sat side by side a man came along and requested a dance. But there was one snag, he was cross-eyed. We were in a dilemma as we were unsure which of the two of us he was expecting to dance with. Anyway my sister got up and away they went so she had made the right decision.

During the evening, sitting opposite to us was this dark haired handsome man constantly staring at me. Eventually he came over to ask me to dance with him. It was not until the last Waltz was announced that he moved very swiftly towards me, bowed and held out his arms to swing me on to the dance floor. While we were dancing the usual questions were asked, my name, where I lived and so on and could he see me again. To all these I refused an answer as somehow I felt a little uneasy about him.

Some weeks later I was taking a stroll along one of the lanes when suddenly a red sports car drew up and who should get out of this car but the man from the dance. He requested me to take a drive with him but in no way was I going to accept such an offer and told him in no uncertain tones and walked off. At a later date he passed my home no doubt hoping I would see him. He had certainly wasted no time in finding out who I was and where I lived.

In later months he came back into my life but there is another story to relate before my friendship with him.

On one of my many visits to Horncastle I was introduced to a man called Mansel. He and his father were painters and decorators. Apparently his father and my father had attended the same school so at least there were no obstacles put in our way to prevent this friendship.

Right from the beginning we got on well together, both liking the same things. We both loved dancing and would attend dances in the Drill Hall in Horncastle. I particularly remember the New Years Eve Territorial Ball. For this occasion I wore a long pink and green net evening dress with lots of layers of net. That evening the music played was by Mantovani and his Tipica Orchestra which added sweetness to our ears. As we danced together Mansel held me close to him and we only had eyes for each other. There was something so mystic about this evening together. It was not until the special feature of the evening was announced that we both returned from Paradise.

What a wonderful sight to behold as we watched the gallant young men of the Lincolnshire Regiment put on a fantastic show. Dressed in their colourful red jackets with white lanyards and with their partners they danced the Mazurka, the Lancers, the Barn Dance and lastly the Military Two-Step. When the clock chimed Midnight we all gathered around this great hall, joining hands and singing *Auld Lang Syne* and wishing each other a Happy New Year.

I felt sad when at 2 a.m. the last Waltz was announced and it was time to go home. I could have danced all night. I was Mansel's Cinderella and he my Prince Charming.

Sometimes we would travel by bus to Lincoln and spend the day looking round the shops, and sometimes we took a stroll up the steep hill to the Cathedral before going to the Theatre in the evening.

Unquestionably one of Europe's finest Cathedrals, Lincoln remains peaceful and unspoilt. Its setting in a close of mellow gateways, old walls and infinitely varied houses lends an air of relaxed timelessness. It is rather strange that during the romance with Patrick, the Rector's son, I visited the home of Alfred Lord Tennyson and now here I was amidst the serenity of the lawns and gardens which extends to the cloisters of the Cathedral when suddenly Mansel and I approached the statue of the very same poet which in a way completed the tranquillity of this ancient setting. It was almost as if the very renowned poet was part of my love life.

At the foot of his statue is one of his poems.

> *Flower in the crannied wall*
> *I pluck you out of the crannies*
> *I hold you here, root and all, in my hand*
> *Little flower – but if I could understand*
> *What you are, root and all, and all in all*
> *I should know what God and man is.*

The symbol of the City of Lincoln is the stone figure of the Cheeky Imp – a stone carving high up in the Angel Choir of Lincoln Cathedral. There are several legends concerning the Imp but the following are perhaps the most interesting.

"The coming of Bishop Remigius to Lincoln made the devil very angry, for up to that time he had had it all his own way in the town and district. The devil tried his utmost to turn him from his purpose of building a cathedral, but without success. At last in desperation – the Minster then nearing completion – the devil waylaid the bishop at the south-western corner of the building and tried to kill him. But the good prelate in his extremity called for aid upon the Blessed Virgin Mary – to whom the Church was to be dedicated – whereupon, the Blessed Virgin sent a mighty rushing wind, which, catching the devil, so hustled and buffeted him, that he slipped inside the Church for safety, where he has been ever since, nor dare he come out, knowing that the wind awaits his return in order to make an end of him."

"The wind and the devil being on a friendly tour, arrived at Lincoln Minster, where the latter addressed his friend thus, "just wait outside while I go in and have a chat with my friends the Deans and Canons". "All right", said the wind, and he has been waiting there ever since! Most certainly the wind on the calmest and sultriest day may always be there felt if not seen; but what may be the inference from the devil's long stay with his friends inside?" (Whites' Lincolnshire.)

"One day, many years ago, the wind being in a playful mood, brought two Imps to see Lincoln. The first thing that attracted their attention on drawing near the City, was its magnificent Minster. They were filled with awe and astonishment at so noble a building, and it caused their hearts to sink within them for a time, but plucking up courage, they flew thither to more closely examine its wonderful carvings and mouldings. After flying around for some hours, one Imp found the south door open and with great trepidation, impishly popped his head inside. Catching sight of the exquisite Angel Choir, he could not resist the temptation of a chat with the angels, so in he hopped, making straight for a pillar, he hopped still higher, but his curiosity cost him dear, for no sooner had he reached the top to rest, than he was in a moment turned to stone. The other Imp, tired of looking for his lost brother, alighted on the back of a witch. He also was immediately turned to stone. The wind still haunts the Minster Close awaiting the return of the Imps." (From a card sold in the Old Cathedral Store, Exchequer Gate.)

That Easter Mansel bought me a huge Easter Egg with a lovely red silk rose on the top which later on I wore on some of my evening dresses.

Sometimes we went into Derbyshire and enjoyed a day there. On one occasion we went to the Horse Racing Meeting at Market Rasen. Another day was spent in Tattershall Castle. This too is one of the landmarks of Lincolnshire so near to Coningsby and Woodhall Spa yet it escaped the bombing of the surrounding villages. The Castle was built in about 1440 by Ralph Lord Cromwell, Treasurer of England under King Henry VI. It consists of five levels and a battlement walkway 100 feet high from where spectacular views can be obtained. The stateroom has a beautiful carved stone fireplace. Surrounding the Castle is a double moat, home of ducks and water fowl. At one time peacocks could be seen strutting across the lawns. On one occasion we climbed the endless narrow stone steps to reach the top and we were almost out of breath. From this height I decided to drop a fountain pen quite expecting to find that it would be damaged but to my amazement it was in perfect condition.

Sometimes we would wander through my father's fields and stand on the bridge over the River Bain and watch the fish swimming downstream. When darkness fell, the moon showed itself shining down on the water. There was a lovely peaceful atmosphere as we snuggled close to each other amidst such romantic surroundings. At that time I was too happy even to think that in the very near future fate was to play a major part to destroy this happiness.

In the Spring of that year Mansel won some money in a sweepstake and out of the blue announced that he had found another girl, a blonde, and did not wish to see me again. There is a saying that men prefer blondes, so being a brunette I did not stand an earthly chance. I was absolutely devastated. I asked myself how could he do this to me? I was beside myself and cried and cried, my world crumbled at my feet. Naturally my parents wanted to know what was wrong and like me they could not believe that this man could treat me so. In the end I came to the conclusion that perhaps she gave to him what I was not prepared to give. Who knows? We naturally discussed sex but he knew my views on this. No way was I ever going to give my body to any man before marriage. In any case there was too much at risk and I had no intention of ever bringing disgrace on to my parents. To be pregnant and unmarried in those days brought stigma with it and everyone looked down on the family. I loved this man dearly and I thought he returned the compliment but how mistaken I was.

The weeks passed by and gradually the hurt was not so great and I could begin to smile again. My friends would say, "There are more pebbles on the beach!" and one day you will find another boyfriend. This seemed far away from my thoughts at this time. Of course my parents were very concerned about my unhappiness and one day suggested that I should go with them that evening to a dance in the Drill Hall at Horncastle. It seemed so strange to go without a partner but we had only been in this vast hall a short time when who should appear in front of me but the man with the red sports car who I had so often rebuked in the past. For him it was a great opportunity to get to know me. Here also was a chance to put the past behind me and grab what future happiness was on offer.

We danced, we chatted and at last I promised to see him again and we arranged that he would pick me up on the following Sunday.

When Sunday arrived I informed my parents of my intentions of going out, to which my father said, "I hope it is not with the fellow you were dancing with the other night. I don't like him. He is a wrong-un". Naturally I did not heed my father's warning. Quite the opposite really. At 3 o'clock prompt there was a hoot for me to show myself.

We travelled to Skegness, visited an aunt of his who invited us to stay to tea. To impress me, I am convinced, was the only reason he took me to Church that evening. Still, he had everything to offer me, a nice car, his own business and lots of entertainment. Now Ray belonged to Boston Motor Club and invited me to go along with him to a dinner and dance in Boston. When I told my father I was attending this dinner and dance he just saw red. Consequently we had a jolly good row but I made it quite clear that I was not changing my mind. Anyway I asked my father to give me one good reason why he so objected. To which he replied that this man would see that I had plenty to drink and then have his way with me. He said that he trusted me but not this man.

From time to time my sister Lily who was really well off would send me some of her lovely evening dresses. For this occasion she sent me a lovely long black evening skirt and a gorgeous silver and black lamé blouse.

Somehow I did not enjoy that evening. In the background of my mind I felt unhappy because I had quarrelled with my father when after all his main concern was for my welfare. Still I continued my friendship with Ray Somehow I had two things to prove. One was for my father's benefit, that perhaps he was very wrong about this man and the other was to prove that if I ever met Mansel whilst out with Ray then I would show him he was not the only pebble on the beach.

I must say that at times Ray took a lot of understanding. For instance I once wore a lovely long white evening dress to a dance in Skegness where we joined many of his friends. That evening he made it quite clear that he did not like the colour of the dress, although he liked the dress. So to please him I persuaded my mother to dye it a pretty mauve. This dress I wore to the theatre in Louth. To me we both looked very smart, he with his evening dress suit, but during the interval he said to me, "Whatever possessed you to dye that lovely white dress mauve?" When it came to day-wear he preferred to see me in a beige gaberdine coat and Reslaw hat and brown walking shoes.

On one of his visits to my home he crossed over to the vase of flowers and touched them. I had arranged some artificial flowers with some greenery from the garden. When we were alone he appeared very cross and said "Fancy deceiving anyone in doing a thing like that". Then I really put my foot in it. His mother became ill, so I picked her some pale wood violets that do not give off any perfume and sprayed them with Ashes of Violet perfume. He went absolutely berserk. Now I ask you, how many men would know that pale wood violets lack perfume? At times life seemed almost impossible with him. Yet he could also be very charming towards me.

During this time I had a letter from Mansel asking if I would see him again. I suggested he should pick me up from my home one evening. Well, he arrived and off we went in his car just down the road. He drew into a gateway and we talked for quite a while. Eventually he asked me to go back to him. But my pride prevented me from agreeing and I told him that he had really hurt me and wouldn't get another chance.

As my life has ticked away I have realised that you can love more than one man. I loved the man I eventually married but in a different way and even told him of the great love that I had had for Mansel. This kind of love was to me the real love of my life. Yet I let it pass me by when I had the chance to re-light the flame of my first real love.

Somehow the friendship with Ray lacked the sincerity of my life with Mansel. Perhaps my father's warning was at the back of my mind and in my every movement. Naturally I was attracted to him, he had good taste when it came to the choice of pictures, theatre and dances. The unhappiness caused by the loss of Mansel made me somewhat disillusioned in men.

Sometimes I asked myself why on earth I turned Mansel's offer down for this man. Yet I continued to see him. There are many lessons to learn in life and this friendship with Ray proved one thing to me. If ever I fell in love again then this man would have to prove a greater love for me.

Ray was a strange man really. The fact that he owned a general store but never once gave me a box of chocolates. In fact I am convinced that he admired me but was too proud to admit it. Or it may have been that for so long I had rebuffed his advances. He was very conceited and maybe he wanted to prove to himself that I too would fall for him. No doubt it became a challenge to him that eventually I should no longer refuse his advances.

Eventually a few days prior to the Coronation of King George VI he announced that he was going down to London to celebrate this occasion. His excuse for not inviting me was that I might faint from the heat of overcrowding. I had previously fainted on one of our visits to Cadwell Motor Cycle Races not from heat but from intense cold. This was really most unfair as on this particular Good Friday meeting when we set off I was feeling a little unwell. In spite of this he had the hood of the car down and once we took our position on the hillside to watch the racing it began to snow. Suddenly without any warning I was in oblivion and when I came back to normal I was aware that I was in the St. Johns

Ambulance Tent once more feeling warm and ready to enjoy the racing. Cadwell Park is a picturesque racing circuit set in attractive grounds between Horncastle and Louth and has been a popular venue for both competitors and spectators since 1930. Each year it hosts race meetings on most weekends from February to December in which top British riders and drivers compete in some of the country's finest motor cycle, car, kart and rally cross events.

Although I joined in the plans for the village celebrations in readiness for the Coronation I naturally felt hurt because of Ray. Everywhere flags and bunting were flying. The coronation of King George VI was made more memorable to our little community because of the Dymoke family who lived close by in a little hamlet called Scrivesby. The line of the King's Champions were descended from this family. Lincolnshire has had since the days of William the Conqueror a special connection with the Kings and Queens of England through the Manor of Scrivesby which is held by the office of the King's Champion. The Champion to William I was Robert the Dispenser who was followed by the family of Marmion and then by the intermarriage of the Ludlows and Dymokes. The Honourable the King's Champion appeared at the coronation from the reign of Richard II to George IV. His duty was to ride into Wesminster Hall, throw down the gauntlet thereby challenging the world to contest the right of the King to the throne.

His perquisite after the ceremony was the Gold Cup in which the King pledged his health. If he had to fight then he could also claim the horse which he rode and the armour he wore which were supposed to be the second best suit and charger in the King's possession.

The challenge has never been taken up, perhaps because of the risk of losing one's head. There is however a tradition that at George III coronation the gauntlet was picked up by a lady who left in exchange another glove with a message that a suitable champion would appear if given a fair field to challenge the King's right, presumably for the Jacobite cause.

The Marmions and Dymokes held large estates in the county of Lincolnshire including parishes in Horncastle. The ancient Manor House Scrivesby Court was twice burnt down.

The present Champion the Honourable Frank Scaman Dymoke had the honour of bearing the banner of England at the coronation of Edward VII and George V.

On May 12th 1937 as the day dawned I realised that by now Ray would be taking up his position in London to watch the splendour of the Royal Procession and I was left behind and feeling a little sad. But during the morning a florist appeared and handed me a lovely bouquet of red roses and on the card the message was "Lots of Love, Ray".

I was absolutely elated, in fact this was the only time that he had ever shown any sign of caring for me. This made my day and I soon joined in the festivities.

In the evening there was a concert in the Church Hall and many of the villagers took part. Tea had been served in the Village Hall so this had to cleared up in readiness for the concert. On this occasion I dressed up as a man in my tails and top hat and white silk scarf and swinging my stick as I wobbled on to the stage I sang:

Show me the way to go home
I'm tired and I want to go to bed
I had a little drink about an hour ago
And it went straight to my head
Wherever I may roam
O'er land or sea or foam
You will always hear me singing this song
Show me the way to go home.

It seems I was a great success. Naturally I had tucked my hair under my hat and some of the local people were unaware that I was this drunken man on the stage.

After all the festivities had died down I took stock of myself and realised it was time I did something more positive with my life. Nursing was the only profession I really fancied. Although to have been a vet and to work with animals would have been my first choice, this was totally out of the question. Having left school at fifteen I lacked many qualifications and furthermore my father could not afford to support me whilst I was training. Actually I did not want to go too far from home as my mother suffered with heart trouble and was unwell at times, so I applied to a hospital in Boston and on the recommendations of both the Headmistress of the School and the Rector I was accepted.

The ancient fenland port of Boston is steeped in history. It was from here that the Pilgrim Fathers were thwarted in their first attempt to flee the country. The cells in which the Pilgrims were imprisoned can still be seen at the Guildhall. On the banks of the River Witham stands the picturesque Maud Foster Mill, the tallest working windmill in the United Kingdom. The tower of St. Botolphs Church, known as *the Stump*, stands out as a great landmark in the flat fenland country. Underneath the tower is a memorial to the five men from Boston who became Governors of Massachusetts.

It did not take long to get into the routine of the hospital. I felt absolutely super in my uniform and the other nurses made me welcome and we had some happy times in the Nurses Home. There was just one snag. I was warned about a certain Staff Nurse who, when a new nurse arrived, constantly pestered her to go into Boston to have a meal. No one liked her, so I too declined her request, but as time went on perhaps she waited for the opportunity to get her own back. For instance Matron sent for me one day and said that she had been informed that I never arrived on duty on time. Naturally I told her I was always on the ward at least ten minutes before the due time. The days passed by and everything seemed fine until once more the Matron sent for me.

This time she asked me if I was the one sitting in a car with my boyfriend outside the hospital gates as he brought me back from my day off. This was correct but as the car was on the main road it did not seem possible that she could complain. Anyway in no uncertain words she made it quite clear that her nurses were not allowed to do this and in future I was to say my good night very briefly and for the car to move on.

Someone it seems had it in for me and there was just one person on whom I could lay my finger. The Nurses' Home was getting too small to accommodate the influx of new

nurses and volunteers were requested to sleep out. I think my hand was the first one to go up. They say, "Big Brother is Watching You" but in my case it was Big Matron. Several of us were moved to a house opposite the Boston Docks and here we felt safe from prying eyes, or so we thought.

Each patient was put into the Recovery Room once their operation was over. Every nurse had the job of sitting with the patient until he or she regained consciousness – baby sitting we called it. My first experience of this was when a young man was slowly recovering from an operation on the middle finger of his left hand. Suddenly he said to me, "Kiss me". Of course I did not kiss him, I just sat there absolutely stunned. Then, because I would not kiss him, he said, "Bugger you". Just imagine if I had kissed him as Matron walked through the doors. I dread to think of the outcome. When he actually came round I told him what he had been saying and we had a jolly good laugh.

One Sunday evening at about six o'clock the patients were given a hot drink and a light meal. In one corner of the ward was a lovely little boy, about nine months old. One of the nurses had fed him and nestled him down to sleep. But on checking him a little later he was found to be dead. Sister was sent for and everything possible was done to revive him but to no avail. A post-mortem was held and apparently he had choked on his vomit. Next morning Sister called we nurses who had been on duty the night before to her office. She told us no blame whatsoever was on our shoulders. We had acted promptly in calling her. She then told us that he would never have walked and that perhaps it was kinder that his little life had been taken to save him many years of suffering.

Looking out of my bedroom window one day I saw one of the nurses on the pavement below so I called to her. She shouted back that she was going shopping and did I need anything, whereupon I retreated into my room, found a handkerchief and tied my money in it and threw it to the ground. Oh! yes after this incident it was back on the red carpet again. Matron knew everything that had taken place that morning and I was well and truly reprimanded. What a vast difference between today's nursing profession and the restrictions laid down in my days.

There is even more – the plot thickens. One of the patients, a nice young man, had written to his brother who was serving in the Forces out in India and told him how nice I was and gave him my name. Consequently I received a letter from him. This letter I showed to the other nurses as we sat having our morning coffee in Sister's room. When she came in we were laughing and she requested to join in. I handed her the letter. She read it, handed it back to me and then stalked out of the room. She went straight to this man's bedside and told him off for disclosing my name to his brother. In fact she was not satisfied with this and she waited for visiting time and told his parents that I was not to receive further letters from India. Perhaps she meant well really and was protecting the welfare of her staff. Not long after this incident I became ill and was sent home to see my own doctor who diagnosed appendicitis, so I was sent post haste to Lincoln hospital to have an operation. For three months I was convalescent and then returned to duty at the hospital.

During this time Ray would call for me on my days off and we would drive into Boston and park the car and wander around the shops. The open air auctions were held on a Wednesday and Saturday. If I was lucky enough to have either of these days off then we would watch the farmers as they unloaded their stock for sale. There was a time when Boston was England's premier port. Many ships arrived with timber from other countries. Trade through the port has brought much prosperity into this area over the centuries. Sometimes we would stroll along to the Guildhall Museum where the Pilgrim Fathers were imprisoned in 1607. On other occasions we would spend time in one of England's largest Parish Churches, the very famous Boston Stump, then off for a meal and afterwards to the pictures.

I think Ray liked to feel that I was taking up a profession and he made sure that if he introduced me to any of his friends they were aware I was a nurse. In a way he was conceited and thought highly of himself.

Perhaps he thought all the girls fancied him. For instance, Matron allowed the nurses to have a party in the Nurses Home and we could invite one guest, male or female. Of course I invited Ray. Would you believe it, under my very nose he danced several times with one of the other girls and asked her to go to the pictures with him the following evening. She told me this the next morning as we went on duty. As she had a lot of respect for me it seems she had flatly refused him. Naturally I tackled him about this incident and the only reaction I had from him was that he was just testing her out to see if she would accept. Her opinion was that like Joseph he had a coat of many colours and that if I would take her advice then he should be sent on his way.

Somehow my plans for the future were jeopardised. I never finished my nursing training, as my mother was taken very ill and I had to return home to look after her and my father. One day I told my mother of the incident of the night of the party at the Nurses Home. This gave her the opportunity she had been waiting for to warn me about the way in which Ray was using me. A friend of my mothers had a relative living a short distance from where Ray lived with his mother and sister. It seems he did not go alone to the coronation but took another girl. My mother suggested that I went to a Boxing Match at Boston where it was more than likely he was sitting with another girl.

Off I went and watched the door as people came in. Lo and behold! there he was with another girl. There was no alternative but to bring this friendship to an end. My father was right after all but I did not wish to believe him. There really was little sadness in my heart over this affair. Because I had previously been jilted it suited me to be this man's girlfriend to overcome the heartache of losing the man I really loved. He just filled a gap in my life and it was nice to be taken to dinners and dances.

In fact it was nice to be back at home with my parents and to see my friends again. Looking after my father and mother and coping with the household chores kept me very busy.

Aunt Lily, David's sister, ran the Post Office in a hamlet called Kirkstead. The main railway lines from Lincoln to Boston passed through this tiny community, and it was well known to travellers as Woodhall Spa Junction. Many years previously my aunt was listening in to the Cat's Whisker radio with her earphones on when suddenly she was struck by lightening and lost the sight of one eye. From time to time she would send an S.O.S. for me to go and take over the running of the post office. In those days I had to be sworn in before I could proceed with any postal business.

Every morning I took a cup of tea up to both my aunt and uncle, butevery morning Aunt Lily always complained that the tea was far too weak. I made up my mind that the next morning she would get a really good strong cuppa. The tea was well brewed and up I went. I put the tea cup and saucer on the table at Aunt Lily's side of the bed and quickly retreated down the stairs. Suddenly came the expected yell, "Do you call this tea? I just cannot drink it." "What is wrong with it? I thought you liked it strong", I said in a very coy sort of voice. To which she replied, "You know just what I mean. Please bring me another cup of tea and I won't ever complain again".

Once Aunt Lily was better she wandered along to the lavatory at the bottom of the garden. Oh! what a laugh. As she entered the kitchen door her skirt was tucked into her big blue bloomers showing her bum. I was almost tempted to let her go into the shop like this but gave it second thoughts and declined.

My Uncle also had a nephew who was a private detective in Nottingham and he turned up one Sunday whilst I was there. He seemed quite attracted to me and after tea invited me to go for a drive in his new car. The following Tuesday he turned up again and on this occasion he asked me to go to the Tattoo at Nottingham that evening. Somehow he did not appeal to me and I declined any further advances.

Meanwhile his mother was getting quite concerned because he was so attracted to the niece in question. Apparently she spoke to Aunt Lily of her concern, to which Lily replied, "You need have no worries about this affair, I will see to it myself that my niece does not marry your son". In later years he married a police woman. This was not a happy marriage as she preferred not to have any children and he was quite the opposite. I actually saw him once again during the War when shopping in Horncastle and he was so delighted to see me. Perhaps he thought he could renew an old friendship but this was not on as I was by then married with a son of my own.

The second victim to be claimed by the River Bain was a farmer called Jackie Richardson who tied a stone weight from the barn around his neck and threw himself into the river and drowned.

This incident shocked the whole village but he was a very unhappy man. His son Stanley was a great disappointment to him. He was the only child and his father had high hopes of him becoming a farmer. But Stanley had other ideas. His talents would have been wasted on a farm so he followed his heart and aimed for bigger things.

Some Sunday evenings my mother and father would take me with them to visit the Richardson family at the farm. Stanley would be upstairs in his bedroom studying and would only show himself at supper time. He would grab two slices of bread and butter and a large Spanish onion and a mug of coffee and then return to his bedroom.

The discovery and development of wireless was among the most wonderful achievements of modern science. My first experience of this brilliant discovery was when I was about eight years old on these visits to the Richardson's.

There was only one set of earphones so we had to take it in turns to listen in. I was absolutely fascinated to listen to the music once the headphones were placed in position. These early wireless sets had a crystal detector. It had been found that certain mineral crystals in conjunction with a needle-point known as a Cat's Whisker possessed the property of unidirectional conductivity or rectification. Later on it was more usual to have a valve for this purpose. It really was a luxury to possess one of these Cat's Whisker wireless sets.

Stanley Richardson went on to Cambridge and eventually became interpreter to Sir Winston Churchill during the Second World War. He was a tall fair haired young man. He too was disappointed that his father could not appreciate his finer qualities and be aware of his brilliance. Although his mother was just homely and comely she worked hard amongst her poultry, producing eggs for sale, selling butter etc. to provide money for Stanley's education. But in the end his father sacrificed his life for nothing. Stanley's life was short too. He was tragically killed in the Café du Paris in London on one of the fierce bombing raids.

His mother was comforted by everyone in the village. Hers had been a sad life, experiencing two miscarriages before Stanley was born.

The school house was too big for Muriel Lamming, the head mistress, so she kindly offered Mrs Richardson a lounge and bedroom with use of the domestic facilities.

One day as she returned from shopping in the town of Horncastle she was very bemused. Apparently she had been into Boots the Chemist and her purchases happened to be a pound of Epsom Salts (I think we all know what they are generally used for) and two toilet rolls. She could not understand why the assistant had such a smirk on his face when she placed her order. It was not until she was opening the door to go out of the shop that she realised why he was smiling. They were not for what he had imagined, she suffered with her feet and Epsom Salts was a good remedy to ease the aches and pains.

five
SECOND WORLD
WAR

*T*he winter of 1939 and 1940 brought with it rain, hail, snow and biting winds. In fact, the River Witham was frozen solid and one could skate from Woodhall Spa to Boston. It takes extreme frost to freeze a river.

Snow and ice had to be removed from aircraft and the runways cleared before take off on many airfields. There were huge drifts of snow some five feet high. To the extent that when those in my father's fields began to thaw the scene was typical of the Arctic – not a hamlet in Lincolnshire. Everywhere you looked there were huge boulders of ice which took many weeks to melt away. Each evening a party of us would meet on the village green, then trudge at least a mile to skate on a disused pit.

A tragedy occurred, no doubt due to these arctic conditions, which shocked the whole village. One evening the miller and baker made his usual routine check of the sluice gates before retiring to bed. Suddenly he slipped on the ice on the bridge which crossed the River Bain, hit the fence, some of which collapsed, consequently throwing him into the freezing water of his own mill pool and he was drowned. He therefore became the third victim to be claimed by the River Bain.

Many wreaths were sent in sympathy. I went along with the family wreath and was invited by Maud, the miller's wife to see Arthur as he lay in his coffin. At a time like this one could not cause offence by refusing her request. Arthur looked so peaceful but the thing that intrigued me was that when he was at work he always kept a pencil above his right ear under his cap and there remained the very signs of the position of this pencil.

In spite of all this sadness life had to go on. An attractive young Head Mistress named Muriel lived at the School House which was across the road from my old home. She was appointed Head Mistress of the School in 1937 and took an active part in the entertainment of the village.

In December of 1939 she requested my help with a forthcoming Nativity Play and dance in the Village Hall. Our first encounter with the boys in khaki was on the night of the play when suddenly the lights went out on the stage

The Mill at Kirkby-on-Bain

causing such a dilemma. I suggested we go to the soldiers/airmen and seek help. Two of them soon volunteered, one named Reg and the other Bill and after a while the lights were back on.

After the play, the room was cleared and seats were put around the hall in readiness for dancing. Firstly refreshments were served and the boys in khaki were invited into the kitchen. Most of my evening was taken up dancing with Reg. When the dance was over and both Muriel and I locked up for the night who should we see again waiting outside but Reg and Bill. As they had left their car at the end of the road just beyond our homes they walked along with us. Of course, they asked to see us again.

At that time I could see the funny side of suggesting we asked them to meet us both on the Village Green at 7 o'clock the following Sunday to go carol singing around the village with the Rector's wife. We said good night and off they went and we had a good laugh as we were convinced we had seen the last of them, we thought that the idea of being under the supervision of the Rector's wife would put them off.

But no, lo and behold, on the Sunday evening as we all assembled on the Village green we could hear the chugging of their little old Austin as it came through the village and out stepped Reg and Bill. That evening I realised that Reg had a good singing voice but was not so sure about Bill. When we reached an outlying farm where Colonel and Mrs Gibbs resided we were invited in to have a mince pie and a hot drink. After we all broke up to return to our homes again Reg and Bill asked to see us again, whereupon to test them out to see what kind of men they were I suggested they came to the Wesleyan Chapel to a social evening on the following Wednesday. Once more they turned up. Reg won the passing -the-parcel and won three tablets of toilet soap which he gave to me.

Our next surprise was an invitation to a dance in the ballroom of the Golf Hotel, Woodhall Spa, which had been requisitioned by the Army at the commencement of the War. In spite of the War being on we wore long evening gowns. I was aware that Bill was not the man for Muriel and they did not meet up again. Reg and I on the other hand were very suited to each other. Whenever possible he came to see me. We would attend dances in the village or go to see a picture showing at the Kinema in the Woods.

The Kinema in the Woods is in use even to this day, though changes have taken place over the years. A vestibule was added on to the front of the cinema and a partition was erected between the foyer and the auditorium. In 1986 a Mr James Green bought and installed a Compton Theatre Organ which had previously been played in a cinema at Charing Cross Road, London.

Reg Simmons

At the time I visited this cinema there were at least six rows of deck chairs at the front, the price around 3/6 but if you sat in one with your boyfriend it was most uncomfortable to even hold hands let alone to lean over to have the odd kiss or two. These deck chairs were followed by rows of most comfortable plush seated tip up chairs, price per seat 2/6. At the rear were long hard wooden forms at 1/-. In those days the floor was not sloping so those sitting right at the rear must have had difficulty in obtaining a good view of the film.

An iron projection room was built into the back of the cinema which is in use to the present day and is believed to be the only cinema in Britain still using wing rear projection methods. Woodhall Spa holds many happy memories for me.

After I met Reg we not only attended the dances at the Golf Hotel and Winter Gardens but one evening we went along to a ball at the Petwood Hotel. For this very special occasion I wore a gorgeous pale green satin backless evening dress sent to me from my sister Lily in London. I felt a like a million dollars. As a party of us were standing chatting away one of the officers walked over to Reg

Dorothy Rose, aged 22

and whispered something in his ear. Later on he told me what he said and we were highly amused. Reg's surname was Simmons and everyone called him Simmy. The conversation was as such:

"Good evening Simmy. Are you expecting your wife and children over for the weekend?"

Reg was dumfounded as he was single and at first wondered how to answer this one and just said, "No Sir".

Perhaps the Officer thought I was what is commonly called a "bit on the side". Mind you I felt glamorous that night and in fact everyone said I looked glamorous too. Who knows but what he was hoping he could be introduced to me but Reg gave no one a chance to get anywhere near me.

But that night was ruined. When we reached my home Reg said he had something to tell me. Naturally I thought perhaps he really was married. But he said, "I must not deceive you any longer, I am engaged to another girl". I was deeply shocked and livid because up to this time I had thought he was so genuine. I immediately got out of the car and told him not to see me again and ran indoors. Days later a note was pushed through the letter box asking me to give him time to sort things out. Three weeks later a knock came at the door, my mother answered it and came to tell me that it was Reg. At first I thought he had a cheek to come and see me. I stepped outside and closed the door behind me. I had no intention of inviting him into the house. He asked me to go and sit with him in his car as he had something important to say to me.

Apparently he had asked for special leave and had been to his home in Leicestershire. Much to the disgust and disappointment of his mother, brothers and sisters he broke off his engagement as he was in love with me.

We soon became engaged and were married in the Village Church on March 21st 1941, but over the many years that we were married I always felt that I was never really accepted by the Simmons family. One thing was that I was Lincolnshire bred and born and not Leicestershire. When Reg's father died apparently he had promised his mother he would never marry. So as the saying goes I was "in the dog house" from the beginning.

The day before the wedding Lily tinted my hair with henna which brings out all the highlights. During this process my father was looking on with great interest. His hair was greying. In fact he had none on the top but plenty each side of his head. Suddenly he asked Lily to try this method on his hair. But alas! once the towel was removed from his head he was no longer grey but very gingery. In a way it matched his moustache which had not changed over the years. At a glance it was obvious that he had been tinted. Only time would bring him back to his normal colour. Even some of the guests at the wedding looked hard and long at him and at a later date asked me what he was thinking of at his age, to have a tint.

The laugh came when he attended the market at Boston the following Wednesday where he was well known. Before the auctioneer commenced the sale of the poultry he walked over to him, removed his cap, then loudly called out, "Who will make me an offer for this bloody Buff Orpington?" These are chickens of a pale ginger colour. You can imagine that until the colour diminished poor father had to put up with the teasing.

Buff Orpingtons

For my wedding dress I wore a long simple gown in satin with a short veil held with a beaded coronet. My sister Lily was the Maid of Honour and wore a beautiful long pale mauve silk net dress and carried matching anemones. The Page Boy wore a suit with long trousers in navy blue, a replica of the dress uniform of the Bridegroom.

As for the little Bridesmaid she looked so sweet in her long white satin dress and matching bonnet complete with a basket of spring flowers.

My bouquet was something of a disappointment. I had hoped for lilies-of-the-valley but owing to the War these were unobtainable and I finished up with white tulips, as I had requested white flowers and there was very little choice.

On the journey from Leicester one of the cars broke down and this delayed the guests by half an hour. Oh, yes! I was beginning to wonder if at the last moment Reg had changed his mind. Still, at last they all arrived. The ceremony commenced. As a very special favour the then Vicar of Swithland travelled from Leicester with the family guests and officiated at the wedding.

The Reception was held in the Village Hall. About 70 guests were invited. Although the War had been going on for about 15 months when one caught a glance of the wedding breakfast this seemed almost unbelievable.

My father had killed and dressed eighteen chickens which mother had roasted in the oven at the side of the fire. Only two would go in the oven at one time so it was a full day's work cooking them. The ham was quite big and had to be cooked in the large jam preserving pan on the coal fire. Many beetroot were cooked too. Tins of fruit had been collected over the months from the shops in Horncastle. The cream was no problem.

During the meal an incident occurred at one of the side tables where sat two of Reg's Army friends who had travelled from Terrington St. Clements near King's Lynn. One of the sergeants took out what he thought was his handkerchief from his pocket, instead of which it turned out to be a pair of lady's pink frilly knickers. He looked in horror and quickly returned them to his pocket. Some of the guests frowned, some of them smiled and some even dared to laugh whilst Jimmy's face was a deep scarlet. His mates back at the Camp knew he was coming to the Wedding and sought to play this joke on him. Thank goodness the Vicar was at the main table. One wonders what his reaction would have been.

Lincolnshire was noted for its many airfields, the nearest one to my old home was that of Coningsby. This was a quiet little village before the Second World War and its most outstanding feature was the Clock which dates back to the Seventh Century. It has a painted dial, measures sixteen and a half feet in diameter and is reputed to be the largest one handed clock in the World. The dial is marked in such a way that it is possible to tell the time to the nearest five minutes.

Work started on Coningsby Airfield in 1937 but the first bombing raid from here did not take place until 1941 when four Hampdens attacked Cologne. Problems were soon encountered. Bombers had great difficulty in taking off from the grass surface and consequently the Airfield was closed for the construction of concrete runways.

Once it was re-opened in August 1943, the new runways welcomed the special skills of the 617 Squadron, the Famous Dam Busters, under the command of Wing Commander Guy Gibson. From here the Squadron once more took off and on this occasion on September 15/16 1943 attacked the Dortmund – EMS Canal using for the first time the 12,000lb high capacity bomb. But, as with the famous dams raid, the Squadron paid a very high price – only three Lancasters returning from the total force of eight.

A pub named the Lee Gate Inn a short distance from the Airfield made a cosy retreat, for a few hours for the Air Crew. They also frequented Abbey Lodge, a regular haunt since their time at Scampton. Wing Commander Guy Gibson was usually accompanied by his dog Nigger who also liked a glass of beer.

Sadly Nigger was accidently killed whilst his master was on one of the famous Dam Buster raid missions. It was a sad day for Guy Gibson when once more he made a safe return to Scampton from one of his raids and there was no dog to greet him.

In 1944 617 Squadron moved to Woodhall Spa. This was to give the unit better security, much of this site was heavily wooded thanks to a man named Mr Parkinson who in the year 1811 had three ambitions, one of which was to plant a forest which became known as Ostlers Plantation. This provided excellent cover for both aircraft and crew. Strange though it may seem, Woodhall Spa has always

been known as the home of the Dam Busters in spite of being stationed first at Scampton and then at Coningsby. Perhaps the reason was because they took up residence at the well known Petwood Hotel. This hotel was requisitioned by the RAF as early as 1940/41 for both living quarters and mess. It was from this station that both Group Captain Cheshire VC, DSO, DFC and Wing Commander "Mickey" Martin DSO and Bar continued their target marking experiments. The flat countryside of South Lincolnshire, between Woodhall Spa and Tattershall Thorpe, was a perfect site for a heavy bomber station although very close to Coningsby.

Before the First World War Petwood Hotel was named Petwood House and was privately owned by Sir Archibald and Lady Weigall, both very much part of the aristocracy of that period. To commemorate the Jubilee of George V they presented to the village part of the grounds of Petwood House which was to be known as Jubilee Park along with a swimming pool.

Amongst their many visitors were the Princesses Alice and Marie Louise daughters of Queen Victoria, Lady Louis Mountbatten, Lord Scarsdale, Sir Malcolm Campbell, Marquis of Douglas and Clydesdale who was a pioneer airman of the early 30's, and many others.

In those days the Petwood Estate extended for many miles around Woodhall Spa and included the Woodhall Spa Baths, the Kinema in the Woods, the famous Golf Course. Once more arises the name of Mr Parkinson, who attempted to realise another of his ambitions, which was to sink a coal mine. He selected a site which later on became known as the Woodhall Well. He employed men to excavate the site but from the shaft at 40 ft clear salt water came gushing out compelling the excavators to retreat. Later on the work was resumed with shifts of men working day and night until a depth of 100 ft was achieved. But unknown to Mr Parkinson these men carried coal down with them and to spur him on they brought it up convincing him that there was coal there. They convinced him to such an extent that he had the bells of Horncastle Parish Church peal out announcing that coal had been found. Soon though he realised the truth and left the area a broken and penniless man.

The pit remained closed for many years but eventually the water accumulated to the extent that it overflowed. In 1824 the "Magical Waters" were extracted and stored and by 1834 Thomas Hotchkin Esq. who had previously built the Victoria Hotel decided to build a Bath House and Pavilions to accommodate patients. But for the original efforts of Mr Parkinson the Spa water may never have been located. The building of his third ambition, a city, never reached realisation. It is sad to think that he never returned even to receive the "Freedom of Woodhall Spa" which really he rightly deserved.

Woodhall Spa was also noted for its Sterling Hatchery where thousands of chicks were reared and sent all over the country. It was one of the first of its kind to offer sex-linked day old chicks, a complex procedure invented by the

Japanese. Very rarely did anyone get more than the odd cockerel or two when choosing pullets.

It was also noted for being the oasis of Lincolnshire, still with the ambience of Victorian England. There are wooded parks and walks and the Golf Course is ranked 26th in the World.

After several months of uncertainty war seemed inevitable. The German Army had already marched into Poland, armoured columns streamed over the Polish border, bombers attacked towns and railways thus disrupting the whole of the Polish defence. An ultimatum had been sent to Hitler saying that unless his armed forces were withdrawn from Poland, Britain would go to war. No reply was received. So in fulfilment of their pledges Britain, France, Australia and New Zealand declared War on Germany.

On September 3rd 1939 the voice of Neville Chamberlain was clearly heard over the Radio as he declared that we were now at War with Germany. In his speech he quoted, "Everything I have worked for, everything that I had hoped for, everything that I have believed in during my lifetime has crashed into ruins". It was not the best of fighting talk a Prime Minister could give, but everyone was well aware of the sadness in his heart, therefore understanding just how he must have felt at the end of his announcement.

Although ours was only a little village with a population of never more than 300 inhabitants life soon began to change. We very soon became involved, living so near to Coningsby Aerodrome and Woodhall Spa Landing Ground. Troops were moved into the wooded areas close to the village. Many would visit the local pub, attend the village dances in the Church Hall. Here they could obtain home made sandwiches and cakes and tea and, whenever they wished to, sit quietly at the small tables provided and write letters to their loved ones. There was no street lighting in the village so we were accustomed to walking around the village in the darkness of the blackout. Windows in every household had to have suitable blackout curtains or blinds or shutters.

Soon knitting needles appeared on the scene at the meetings of the Women's Guild where socks, scarves and balaclava helmets were made to be sent to our local boys.

The reality of war becomes more urgent in everyday life when members of your family leave these shores to fight the enemy.

On September 10th 1939 under the Command of General Lord Gort Allied Forces began to move to France. Amongst these many Regiments were two of my brothers, Edgar and George. Meanwhile Arthur was not in the forces but like so many contributed to the war effort by using his skills in the Fairey's Aviation Factory at Hayes, Middlesex.

Both Britain and France built up their forces and waited for Germany to take the initiative. Eventually in April of 1940 Germany made its first move which opened up the first campaign by invading Denmark and Norway. Denmark offered very little resistance. Allied Forces were then hastily embarked for Norway. But Germany had too great an advantage, whilst the Allies had no port or air cover, and the German bombers attacked them without respite.

By May 10th of that year the British and French Forces advanced into Belgium to meet the German drive but they were no match for the German armoured columns. In quick succession the Germans took Brussels, Amiens and Antwerp then crossed the River soon reaching the old battlefield of the Somme. Not long after this Boulogne and Calais were also in enemy hands.

The Allied Forces in Flanders were cut in two by the German thrust towards the sea. There was now no alternative but to evacuate as many men as possible from the beaches of Dunkirk.

It became quite clear that the German strength had been sadly underestimated by the Allies. The possibility of retreat was fully understood by the Government, therefore Mr Anthony Eden informed General Gort that the only course open was for the Forces to fight their way back to the West where all beaches and ports East of Gravelines were to be used for embarkation. The Navy would provide a fleet of ships and small boats and the RAF full support.

The Germans harassed the withdrawal unceasingly with bombing and artillery fire. The dive bomber was a new weapon and terrifying. The troops that began to pour onto the Bridgehead were utterly exhausted having had to fight every inch of the way.

Shelled, bombed and machine gunned these soldiers waited patiently, courageously and good humouredly on the beaches for their turn to embark.

There was no panic, no fighting for positions as they waited up to their waists in the sea until the boats came to take them off. The fleet that began to assemble off Dunkirk must have been the strangest gathering of craft that a British Admiral had ever commanded. There were destroyers, cargo boats, fishing boats, yachts, motor boats and even pleasure boats.

George was already safely back in England. He was found in a disused barn suffering from Typhoid fever and brought back. David and Rose Bell received a Telegram to say that he was dead, but he was very much alive. This mistake was soon put to rights. In warfare one has to accept that mistakes are inevitable.

As for Edgar, he along with his mates suffered the never ending attacks from the air. One wonders what his thoughts were when suddenly he saw a rosary on the beach and picked it up and brought it safely back to England. When he returned home I asked him if I could have the rosary and to the present day it has been one of my greatest possessions. This may have saved his life.

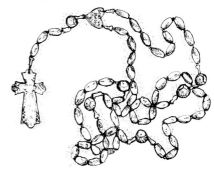

No one knows just how they suffered the agonies of utter helplessness. More prayers no doubt were said than in any other part of the War. Yet the miracle of saving so many lives had been accomplished. The flower of the British Army threatened with annihilation was snatched from the very jaws of the enemy to fight again and to conquer.

Throughout the grim conflict of the Second World War, King George VI and Queen Elizabeth remained with their people, much of the time in Buckingham Palace, though this Royal residence like the rest of London, underwent its ordeal of heavy air attacks by the German Air Force.

On one occasion George VI travelled through Kirkby-on-Bain on his way from Coningsby to Woodhall Spa, no doubt to visit his forces before they went on their respective missions. He also met Field Marshall Montgomery, Wing Commander Leonard Cheshire and Wing Commander Mickey Martin on one of his visits to these two airfields. His visits were usually very "hush hush" although we were aware he visited the airfields in Lincolnshire. No one could have done more than their Majesties to hearten and inspire the people of Britain and the Commonwealth, not forgetting by their well timed messages broadcast in the days of anxiety and stress.

On Sunday May 12th 1941 my little village received its heaviest air raid of the entire War. Houses were damaged, the Wesleyan Chapel destroyed, the post mistress lost the use of her left arm. As she walked downstairs the front door flew open and a piece of shrapnel pierced her arm. One end of my old home was covered in holes also from the blast.

The house just beyond my home had the worst damage, walls crumbling, roof shattered. Yet amidst all the rubble was the chamber pot undamaged and still full! Huge craters were found in the fields the next day. This village seemed to take the brunt of the bombing as the Germans tried to pin point Coningsby and Woodhall Spa. After the raids it was amusing to hear Lord Haw Haw announcing over the radio from Germany. He was heard to say "Germany calling, Germany calling. Coningsby Aerodrome was heavily bombed last night". Only we knew differently.

Sometimes I would cycle into Woodhall Spa. One day while crossing the railway lines between the main gates my bicycle wheel must have caught in a rut, and I was thrown to the ground. It is on occasions such as this that you hope no one is looking, especially as I saw the contents of my handbag scattered everywhere. There was everything in this bag, ration book, identity card, money, a length of string, small narrow bandage, small scissors, safety pins, needle and cotton etc. Everything for an emergency. Who should come to my rescue but two soldiers. They were very kind but I hurriedly grabbed my handbag, thanked them and cycled on my way feeling somewhat silly with having so much junk in my bag.

Other people seem to cope so much better with such things. One day as our family doctor and his wife, residents of Woodhall Spa, were walking down the main street called the Broadway, her knickers fell down to the ground. She calmly stepped out of them, the doctor picked them up and put them into his pocket and away they went unconcerned.

To make the entrance to our little hand gate easier to find in the dark I put about a dozen stones on each side and painted them white. The next time this doctor came to visit my mother he asked me who had painted them. When I told him he replied, "You will be painting the bloody coal next Dorothy". If it was a cold day he would go straight towards the fire, lift up the ends of his overcoat and warm his bottom.

Some weeks before Reg and I were married he was moved to Terrington St. Clements in Norfolk. He sold his old Austin car and purchased a motor cycle as it took less petrol on his visits to me. My mother suffered from heart trouble so it made it easier for me to remain at my home for the duration of the War.

My father represented the village on the Council in Horncastle. At one of the meetings he was asked to find homes for evacuees who might be sent from London. To us it seemed silly at the time because of the air fields. Fortunately for them no refugees finally came, but anyway he had the job of getting a list of people prepared to take one. New people had just purchased a farm about half a mile out of the village and he requested me to go along to them. They were delighted to see me as apart from the postman I was the only one who had paid them a visit. Although they were old enough to be my parents we got on very well together and they invited me to go again. In fact I became a regular visitor. Once they began to know me they would give me a little farm butter now and then which was very acceptable as our ration of butter at that time was just two ounces per person. My father had long since given up farming and just reared some poultry, so my mother would buy extra milk, leave it in a large bowl then skim the cream off and in an evening we would pass a large sealed jar around for everyone to give it a shake until the cream turned to butter.

One day while travelling from Woodhall Spa with dad in his old Wolsely car with a Dickey at the back we noticed a lot of activity on the lane amongst the woodland. We both got out of the car and right before our very eyes was Princess Alice being greeted by the Officers of the Regiment who were standing in great numbers to be inspected by Her Royal Highness. It was snowing like mad and we felt very sorry for the men. One wonders how long they had been standing there. Princess Alice was beautifully attired in a lovely fur coat, matching hat and knee length boots. After the parade she was driven to Petwood Hotel to partake of lunch comprising fresh salmon followed by strawberries and cream.

Once more the allied troops left these shores, this time for the Middle East to take up their arms against the German and Italian forces.

Although General Alexander took supreme command, General Montgomery assumed command of the 8th Army later on to be known as the Desert Rats.

This was a more difficult campaign, not only had the Forces to face the enemy but also the storms of the desert. Apparently a sandstorm in a desert brings terror to both man and beast. At its approach the camels are made to kneel and their masters take shelter beside them, covering their faces to keep out the smothering dust. We who live in the green fields or the paved streets of towns and cities have no idea how blinding a storm can be.

Men of this wonderful Eighth Army, already shaped into an irresistible fighting machine were responsible for one of the great feats in the history of war. Their long and tedious chase along the North African coast resulted in the complete defeat of Rommel, culminating in the decisive Tunisian campaign.

Although toughened by unremitting warfare in the desert they made up a force which was unique in both efficiency and spirit. There remained a human side to them when they paused now and again to smoke a cigarette. For instance I posted out 100 Players cigarettes to my brother Edgar, his favourite cigarettes, but in the same parcel I enclosed some toilet soap. By the time the parcel reached him the cigarettes had become contaminated by the perfume of the soap. He wrote to say that they could not smoke them. This took some believing. What? Stuck out in the desert and not a fag in sight? I am sure he and his troop would have to give in.

But it was not until the night of October 23-24 1942 that the tide turned and everything seemed to fall into place when General Montgomery launched a terrific offensive against the German and Italian Troops facing him at El Alemein. His well equipped army included many new tanks amongst them the Flail Tanks which cleared a way through the mine fields, and his air superiority was complete.

The fighting was intense for at least a week. Eventually in March 1943 these troops blasted a way into Tunisia. The last enemy resistance in North Africa ceased in mid-May.

In many cases the German and Italian prisoners of war respected the British Forces. For instance one German soldier made a statue in white alabaster the size 6" x 5½" with the inscription, "*Lest we forget*", and presented this to Edgar which he brought back to England and which is carefully tended by his wife.

There are times when one would like to hear of the experiences of warfare, even from your loved ones, of the intensity of the fighting. But perhaps they want to forget it and not talk about it. All I remember of Edgar was when he mentioned the Friendly Fire. It was bound to happen, more so in those days than the present day with all the modern technology to hand. The expanse of the sands of the desert is enormous and it was inevitable that there was a greater possibility of the Friendly Fire.

While Edgar was out in the Middle East I gave birth to a son on May 15th 1942 whom his father Reg and I christened John Adrian. His Godmother was Miss Hilda Marsh, the Head Mistress of the school at Kirkby on Bain and his Godfather was her brother, Professor Marsh on one of his visits to the village from Cambridge University.

Soon Reg was sent to a place called Lusaka in Africa to build Prisoner of War camps so he saw little of John until after the War. Although in private life a building contractor he joined the T.A. along with many of the local Leicestershire businessmen and all were called up at the outbreak of the War , their first camp being at Woodhall Spa.

One Saturday evening my father brought home with him a very nice fair haired soldier who turned out to be the officers' cook. He stayed to supper and enjoyed the meal partaking of home made pork pie and haslet. The next day he came along on an old bicycle from the camp site about a mile from the village to request a special favour. He wanted my father to sell him some pork to put on the menu for the officers that night as something special for a change. Naturally, dad selected a piece and gave it to him and away he went. After this he became a regular visitor. Although he knew I was married he said to my parents that he would like to take me to a dance in appreciation of their kindness to him. Naturally my father frowned upon this but left it to my own response to the invitation.

As much as I would have liked to accept I refrained, but did say to him "When I write to my husband out in Africa I will tell him of the situation in question and await his reply".

Eventually the reply came. "Although I trust you, I don't trust any other man and the answer is NO".

Fortunately the regiment left the area so it saved me the embarrassment of telling the soldier the comments in my husband's letter. In fact he seemed such a nice fellow and was just recovering from the shock of losing his wife and baby in childbirth.

The lives that lay ahead for the two men I loved, my husband and my brother, were so totally different.

Reg was out in the land of plenty. Had a boy to do his personal washing and ironing who also slept on the floor at his bedroom door every night to guard him. All he had to do was instruct his men on the erection of huts to house the

prisoners of war. He met a rich farmer and his wife and would stay on at their ranch at weekends enjoying delicious meals and entertainment. He was given a horse to ride but preferred something with an engine and four wheels. Now and again a party of them would go shooting in the bush, hence the arrival of a Lion skin which hung on the wall in the hall for many years.

Edgar, on the other hand, was involved in warfare, facing the sand storms as well as the enemy, and on Army Rations. No doubt he had thoughts of whether he would return to these shores whilst Reg would come back safely unless something unforeseen happened.

Life in the village changed very little. There would be the Saturday night dances in the Village Hall, attended by both soldiers and airmen.

Edgar Cook in 1942

On one occasion as I wended my way home from visiting a friend and widowed mother in spite of it being very dark, I could see figures moving around in the orchard area of my father's garden. I quietly made my way through the gates of the ground surrounding the Village Hall where I could look over the hedge to get a close view of the trespassers. Lo! and behold right before my very eyes were the boys in khaki picking the apples. In a very gruff voice I shouted, "What are you doing in my garden?" The response to this was amazing. Immediately the soldiers began to empty their pockets and throw the apples to the ground apparently more shocked than if they had been on duty where they might have heard something quite different. "STOP! Who goes there? Advance and be recognised. Friend or foe", and so on.

Indeed they would not have enjoyed the apples they had picked as they were Bramley seedlings and used more in cooking. Anyway, I invited them all up to the house and filled their pockets with more appetising fruit.

A newly married couple came to the village to live, he was at least twenty years older than his wife. They seemed quite happy in spite of not wishing to join in the village community, but after the birth of their second child it was obvious that she was suffering from depression. In spite of this they preferred to keep themselves apart from the rest of the village. Time passed by and a third child was born. The husband was a game keeper and left her all day to cope alone. Gradually the children were neglected. Apparently they slept under the kitchen table covered with old coats with only a dimly lit candle, but every Friday night their father gave them a treat. He took them to the bakehouse and purchased all the stale cakes and bread. It gave the baker great satisfaction to see the children's faces light up as they entered the door. The light from the Aladdin lamps just fascinated them and then they had a mad half hour chasing each other around the long troughs.

Eventually the children were taken into care. Meanwhile the mother did strange things. In the heat of the Summer she would walk round the village dressed in many old coats and a big fur hat but speak to no one. One night when it was extremely dark I was walking home from a friend's house when suddenly out from a very high hedge loomed a tall dark figure. I was petrified and almost flew home. Apparently by now my face was quite ashen and dad asked me if I had seen a ghost. I replied that I certainly had. Once I explained what I had seen my parents confirmed that this was happening most evenings to other residents. In a way this in itself was a cry for help and eventually she was cared for in a home.

I would take my usual walk to the farm taking John in the pram. One day Grandma Sexty as we called her, was out in the paddock feeding the poultry. I walked just inside the gate to go towards her when suddenly a Rhode Island Cockerel flew towards me and attacked my legs, bruising them very badly. On my next visit to the farm John and I were asked to stay to lunch. Our main course was the afore mentioned cockerel and all the trimmings. It was decided that he was too dangerous to have around and so he paid the price but made a very tasty meal.

It was lovely to see the family of cats and kittens waiting at the milking parlour door for their much loved dish of warm milk straight from the cows. When they gave me a pound of farm butter to take home with me this was always safely hidden in the well of the pram. Woe betide if we had been caught, there would have been a heavy fine imposed. When you think of our meagre rations then it was no wonder that most of us strayed a little at times.

John and his Grandpa were great pals. They would spend many happy hours in the fields tending the poultry. One day John locked Grandpa in a chicken hut, and jumped for joy as he heard Grandpa calling out, "Let me out!" When he finally decided to let Grandpa out John could not unlock the door. Consequently John ran into the house to find me. When I saw what he had done I gave him a good "telling off", yet there stood Grandpa having a jolly good laugh. He thought it was hilarious.

Sometimes they would have a game of shop, John of course being the shopkeeper. He would go with his order book to Grandpa to get his order. One day Grandpa asked for a pound of candles. to which John replied "I do not keep candles in my food shop, but you can have a gallon of paraffin". What a laugh we all had, smelly paraffin of all things in a food store. This story was related over and over again for many years. The biggest laugh was one Sunday when John returned from Sunday School. He gave each of us one of his story books, put a stool up to the tea trolley and pretended to play as of the organ and said, "Now sing". Suddenly he shouted, "Stop". He knelt down and ordered us to do so, then he began to pray, not in his own voice but in a deep sanctimonious voice typical of a parson, words we were unable to decipher – just a mumble. He then went to his toy box and brought out a tin lid, he came towards us and said, "Put your money in here". His collection finished up in his money box.

The greatest land, sea and air operation in the history of warfare was put into effect on June 6th 1944 when the Allies launched their mighty assault for the liberation of North West Europe. This was no operation of armies alone. Navies, armies and air forces of the British Commonwealth and the United States all took part. In supreme command was the United States soldier General Eisenhower. Once more my brother Edgar left these shores.

Originally the date fixed for the landings in Normandy was June 5th 1944 but the sea was so rough, the cloud so low that at the last minute it was delayed. But on the night of June 5th ships began to assemble ready for the assault. At dawn on the 6th Operation Overlord began. The enemy's defence was strong in patches but it was quite clear that the surprise landing had really achieved its aim. Also the bombing of the previous night disorganised the enemy's communications.

Losses were much lower than expected, but at times like this the waiting for all families everywhere was intense and nerve wracking. The Radio at my home was switched on at all times of the day awaiting news of this great assault. Naturally we said prayers for everyone but a little extra for my brother Edgar.

By June 19th the Normandy Bridgehead was 50 miles long and 12 miles deep and the fortress of Europe had been successfully invaded. Though much stern resistance had still to be overcome the end of the Second World War was at last in sight.

There have been many stories written on World War II but the memory of the Allied Attack on Arnhem during the period of September 17th to the 24th 1944 was the one which in a way affected our everyday life. Movement of troops from the closely guarded woods surrounding our little village made us realise that these men were destined to take part in the realities of war and could no longer enjoy the peace and tranquillity of these pleasant surroundings. The skies at this time seemed to be full of aircraft.

Until we heard the news on the radio little did we know of their mission. British and Polish Parachute and gliderborne troops landed in an attempt to seize the Bridge over the Rhine at Arnhem towards which the British 2nd Army was advancing from the south. Heavily outnumbered by the Germans they fought for eight days and nights to keep a foothold in the town until reinforcements could reach them. But all efforts to relieve them failed and the survivors had to be withdrawn across the river during the night of September 25th/26th.

It was heart-rending to listen to the news, to hear that the Germans were using flame throwers on these men as they tried to cross the river. They were just human torches. As we sat around listening to the radio there was not a dry eye amongst us. Even my father was red eyed. Some of these men had visited the local pub, and played darts, snooker and cards in the Village Hall.

There was sadness and joy when at last the War was over. Some had lost sons, some husbands, some their sweethearts and they must have felt very sad. Yet here was I so lucky to have the return of both my loved ones, my husband Reg and by brother Edgar.

Sydney, the boy previously mentioned having lost the sight of one eye from a homemade firework, had become a fine fellow and in spite of his disability he was accepted in the Forces. During this time he was taken ill with Tuberculosis and died very suddenly. The Army Authorities brought him home to be buried but his father lived in a tiny cottage with just a living room and a kitchen and one bedroom above. So he sought permission from the Rector to have Sydney spend the night before the burial in the church to which the Rector readily agreed.

As he laid in his coffin all alone my thoughts went back to the happy times we had had as children and wondered if he, although dead, was aware of the times that red dotted handkerchief had been tied to the church door. To me there was a special warmth reaching out to him. Once when on leave from the Forces he quietly told me that he would have liked to have asked my hand in marriage but felt he was not good enough, but to me he was more like a brother.

Although you may touch someone when they are in their coffin they feel so cold to your finger tips but no one knows if they are fully aware of your presence. In fact some people say it is better to touch someone then you will never remember the sad days but all the happy times spent together.

Several years later Edgar suffered a great setback – he suddenly went blind. He was rushed off to hospital, sadly there was little that could be done to save his sight. His retinas were detached and the weakness may have been caused by the sands of the desert. He was blind for 15 years until out of the blue a surgeon suggested another operation. He had nothing to lose and agreed to this taking place. The next three weeks were an anxious time especially for his wife Olive and for me and our friends and relations. What joy when we were told the operation was a success and he could see once more.

After the war Reg and I were invited to the wedding of his Sgt. Major Charles Sibson and his bride to be Doris. At the reception I was shown to my seat and sat down and I could not believe the name on the card of the guest who would by occupying the seat next to me. The very Captain who I had seen in the ballroom at the Petwood Hotel who may have thought I was a bit on the side.

I smiled to myself as I thought this would become a very laughable situation. Charles and Doris were not aware of the incident at the Petwood Hotel. As he had been stationed at Woodhall Spa and I came from the village nearby perhaps they had decided I was the right person to sit alongside him during the reception. Before the Captain sat down he introduced himself whilst I announced that I was Simmy's wife. Actually he must have forgotten seeing me in the company of Simmy and friends or he was a good actor, not in the least embarrassed. In fact I was somewhat disappointed as I had expected quite the reverse.

six
LEICESTERSHIRE

*I*t was not until January 1946 that John and I left my parents' home in Lincolnshire to join Reg in Leicestershire, in the village of Rothley.

Before we could move to Leicestershire a house had to be found. Finally Reg's mother offered us hers on the condition that he built her a bungalow. This was too good an offer to miss so meanwhile we rented a house. Finally the bungalow was available for his mother and at last we moved into her house, which was called *the Byeways*, at the corner of a crossroads. The move was in the nick of time as Cedric our second son was born the following day. As soon as I returned from the nursing home the decorators moved in.

All this was a different lifestyle from that which I had been used to. Suddenly I had a husband and two children to care for and with paint and wallpaper in every room. Eventually everything fell into place and we could settle down to family life. We were still on rations and I found it very difficult to eke out the food. Although we lived opposite a farm from which we bought milk, even this was rationed. In fact one Sunday evening there was only a drop of milk left in the jug until delivery next day and I turned to Reg and said that if only I knew where I could find a cow in a field, even at this time of night, I would have a go and try to get some milk.

We were able to keep Bantams so supplement our egg ration. On one occasion as I approached the pram a bantam hen flew out, and would you believe it, at the side of Cedric's head was an egg, yet he was still asleep.

The garden looked very neglected and on enquiring about a gardener-handy man we were told that if we applied to the Prisoner of War Camp just two miles away, the authorities would permit a German Officer to come and work for us. The condition was that he was not paid, but if we wished we could provide food for him and give him cigarettes.

Well, the day arrived, the front door bell rang and on opening the door I saw this handsome German Officer in uniform who immediately clicked his heels and saluted me. He then pointed to the garden and made gestures as if he was digging. All I could do was to smile and point to express to come this way.

Kurt Bloss, POW.

His name was Kurt Bloss, he was married and had two little daughters who were living in the Russian Zone and from whom he had very little news. He had been a physics teacher in Germany before the war.

He was an extremely nice man with good manners and it did not take him long to cultivate our language. Reg and I invited him to join us at meal times. He insisted on spoon feeding Cedric, thus allowing me to enjoy my meal, before he sat down to his.

One day I asked Kurt to keep an eye on Cedric as he lay in his pram while I went to the village for provisions. When I returned I noticed some washing on the line which was not there when I had left. It seems that Cedric had been kicking away and on "filling his nappy" had spread it around! Without any ado Kurt had taken him to the house, washed him and put on a clean vest and nappy, and then washed his soiled clothes and put them on the line.

To show our appreciation of this man's devotion to duty we decided to take him to the theatre in Leicester. Reg obtained permission for Kurt to stay out until midnight. He could not have appeared in a public place in a German uniform so I kitted him out in one of Reg's suits. I did not really enjoy the performance as I was afraid that we might be found out. It was such a relief when we arrived back at Byeways and Kurt was back in his uniform.

He would tell us of many incidents in his life, but one stands out in my memory. It seems that while he was at university he and his colleagues had to attend a monthly meeting in the presence of the Professor. On the agenda one evening was a discussion on whether to segregate the boys from the girls in separate houses. Right at the start, a house master stood up and asked for permission to speak, which of course was granted. But what he had to say was met with some consternation. Although true to life he explained it rather crudely by saying "If you were to build the highest wall the boys would find means of scaling it. What is more, if the girls were to wear tin knickers the boys would carry tin openers".

Eventually the POWs were sent back to Germany. Naturally we missed not having Kurt around. We corresponded for a while then his letters ceased. Both Reg and I were aware that Kurt intended going into the Russian Zone to rescue his family but this was a very risky escapade at that time. Perhaps he was caught. This has always remained a mystery.

Reg worked long hours trying to get the business back on its feet. There was even a regulation that no one could have any work carried out costing more than £100 in materials. Most afternoons I would take John and Cedric down to Swithland Reservoir to feed the swans and watch the trains as they passed overhead on their journey to Leicester. As time passed by they attended Swithland Infant School. Then in January 1949 a daughter, Helen Joyce, was born. Reg was overjoyed about her birth, more so than at the births of the two boys, she was the "apple of his eye" and remained so until his passing away. Although I was the twelfth child and there had been previously four daughters I too was much loved by my father and to see Reg love Helen so clearly reminded me of the love my father and I shared. Naturally there was a great bond between my mother and me, but I had always been a bit of a Tomboy and loved the farm life and spent a lot of time with my father.

In May of that year my mother died. It is sometimes said that a daughter is sent to replace the loss of your own mother, and having Helen helped to relieve the sadness of my loss. After the death of my mother my father lived alone in part of the cottage and Edgar and his wife Olive in the remainder. Edgar, too, was the only son who really cared about our parents. Maybe this was one reason I admired Edgar so much, as he was so caring.

During the weeks that my mother was ill I travelled back home each week-end to help to nurse her. It seems that on the very week-end on which she passed away I took John with me. I had no choice but to leave Cedric and Helen with relatives.

Sadly on our arrival my father informed me that mother had been in a coma for several days. In spite of this bad news I took John upstairs with me. She looked so peaceful. Quietly I said to her, "I have brought Johnny to see you". She immediately opened her eyes, made a gesture with her left hand towards him, suddenly said "Johnny" then fell back and never spoke another word. On the Sunday afternoon she passed away.

In villages years ago there was always a midwife who was also called in to prepare a dead person for what was crudely called the "laying out". Mrs Spikings arrived and requested certain articles. Once I had supplied her with the necessary items I made my way towards the door but she asked me to stay and help her. It seemed a very sad thing and I almost declined. Looking back over the years I am glad I had the opportunity to help in this way as I know my mother would have wished me to do so. One may never fear death. As she lay there she looked just like the late Queen Mary.

My father never really got over the loss of my mother and perhaps became a little careless. On getting up in the morning the first thing he did was to light the fire and put on the kettle to make a cup of tea, but sadly on the morning of

March 7th 1953 the fire refused to burn so he took it upon himself to fetch the paraffin can and threw some directly onto the fire. This was indeed a stupid thing to do. It could have cost him his life. Flames lapped everywhere and it was not long before the old cottage was burned almost to the ground. He came to live with us for a while but never really recovered from losing the home he had known for so many years. In October of that year he passed away, happy to be reunited with his beloved Rose Bell.

A month later my sister Lily passed away suddenly, at the age of 49 years. This was indeed a shock to her devoted husband and to Reg and me and our three children. Only the week before she and her husband Eddie had come over from Ashbourne in Derbyshire to have lunch with us. For several years she had suffered from Diabetes but she had always enjoyed life to the full and never showed any signs of illness. That week-end she had to retire to her bed with a bout of flu. On the Tuesday Eddie decided to cook her favourite dish of duck for the evening meal. They owned a little pub in Kniveton and on that very afternoon a representative of one of the breweries paid his usual visit. It was an opportune moment for Eddie to pay the account. He took the cash tin up to Lily to count out the amount, meanwhile he popped into the kitchen to make a cup of tea and to check the oven.

On his return to their bedroom he was deeply shocked to find that Lily had collapsed and lay back on the pillow. He took a closer look, spoke to her, but there was no reply. Suddenly a cold shudder hit him as he realised that she had passed away. The uncanny thing about this was that she had counted the correct amount of cash some of which remained in her hand. Eddie telephoned me immediately. Poor man, he was absolutely distraught. What's more, when I was told the sad news I too was deeply shocked. Although it was November and terribly foggy I promised him that Reg and I would be with him as quickly as we could, once we had found a baby sitter for the children.

When we reached Ashbourne the fog was so thick it was impossible to decide which road to take to Kniveton. Whatever road we chose we still came back to the same crossroads. Eventually we made it. On nearing the pub we could see a light. Standing in the middle of the road was Eddie swinging a lantern to show us the way.

Needless to say the journey back to Leicester at two o'clock in the morning was a nightmare. What with the shock of Lily's death and the awful journey there, it was not long before I fell asleep. Suddenly the car swerved, hitting the curb which quickly brought me back to my senses. Reg too was tired after a day's work and driving under such conditions. He too must have dozed off for perhaps only a split second. To keep awake we just talked and talked. What a relief when the car entered the gates and we were back home "safe and sound".

Eddie visited us as often as he could once he found someone to take over the pub for a few hours. Eventually John and Cedric went off to stay with him

John, Helen and Cedric

for a week. Apparently the locals made a great fuss of the two boys. Meanwhile Reg and I, along with Helen, took up the threads of getting back to normal after so much unhappiness.

One day the painter and decorator and sign-writer named Dick, who was employed by our building firm, came to our farm to decorate a bedroom. Usually I made him a pot of tea at lunch time but on this occasion I was going out so I dug out an old electric kettle, and left this, with some tea, sugar, milk and a mug.

Just before I left the house Dick came running down the stairs complaining, "I am sorry I cannot drink my tea as it tastes of perfume". This sounded absolutely ridiculous so we both went upstairs and examined the kettle. Oh yes! we found the reason. Inside the kettle was, of all things, one of my small bottles of a perfume called *Mischief*. Now who could have put it there? "Little Miss Mischief herself – Helen".

Dick had switched on the kettle and as he stood on the tall steps painting the ceiling the steam rose to his nostrils and he said, "To me it was smelling like a theatre stage door, which I really could not understand". No wonder he made such a comment. Perfume is not the thing to put in a kettle. We never found out why Helen had thought of hiding the bottle in there. One cannot imagine what goes on in a child's mind.

For years I had tried to win the affection of Reg's mother but all was in vain. Suddenly she was taken ill during the Christmas festivities in 1951, while staying with her daughter Olive. As Olive had to return to her job after Christmas the question arose, "Who would look after Grandma Simmons?" There were no offers forthcoming from the rest of the family, so I decided to take up the challenge. Perhaps on this occasion I might succeed and the barrier would be lifted.

At that time John and Cedric went off to school each day, but Helen was not yet three years old, so it was quite a big additional responsibility.

In fact, instead of taking breakfast upstairs just for Grandma Simmons it soon became two, as Helen wanted to have her breakfast with her. After several days I noticed a change taking place in the "old lady" to the extent that one day as I was going to remove the tray she caught my hand and said, "I am sorry for the way in which I have treated you over the years. You wanted to become a daughter but you took my favourite son away from me and it is only now that I regret my attitude towards you and I hope you will forgive me".

After this incident we became very close. At least she made her peace with me before she died on 6th February 1952. A day to remember as King George VI also passed away.

During her stay with us she asked Reg to collect her will from the solicitors and when he arrived back with it she asked him to open it and read it to her as she was not very happy about it. But Reg refused saying that the envelope was sealed and would remain so while she was staying with us.

After the funeral the solicitor arrived to read the will. I, for one, preferred not to go into the room to listen to its contents being read aloud. But when Reg came out he looked pale and shocked. He came towards me and said, "She has cut me out of her will, I cannot believe it". Some time later he realised the reason for her requesting the will while she was staying with us. It would appear that she might have changed this will. But we were glad not to have been part of her plan. Had we agreed, the possible backlash from other members of Reg's family could have proven to be extremely uncomfortable for the two of us.

There is a saying, "there is much work for idle hands". In my case I had very few idle hours to myself. Reg's firm were opening up a Sand and Gravel business nearby, and a weigh bridge had to be installed. A retired gentleman from Derbyshire was found to carry out this job. Digs had to be found for him. This was impossible so guess what? I took pity on him and volunteered to take him in. It was not long before he was settled in with us. Very soon he became Grandpa Collins. He was a lovely old gentleman. He had lost his wife some years before and lived with his son and daughter who it seems were really unkind to him.

He was with us for about three months. During his leisure hours he loved to get out on an old bicycle we had in the garage and he cycled around the countryside. Sometimes he would take Helen with him. Reg made a little seat for her which was fastened on to the back of the bicycle. She was only three years old and she just loved it. He always took an apple with him, and they would find a place to sit at the side of the road. Out would come his pen knife (his friend for many years) and they would enjoy the apple. When we took our annual holiday he would return and look after the house and poultry.

The word "poultry" brings to mind a story. Nearby a farmer had a small paddock, with a stack of straw for bedding down his pigs. He also had lots of rats which paid us a visit and of course they ate our eggs. The story goes that one rat will lie on its back holding an egg and another one will pull it along. Sounds totally out of the question but is very true. We dare not put poison down to kill the rats, so Reg decided to reverse the car up to the hen house and put a pipe from the exhaust of the car down the hole and into the run that the rats had made. He started up the car and you may think you can guess the rest. Would you believe it? Reg had forgotten to turf the hens out of the hut first. When he eventually thought of it and opened the hen house door they all came staggering out, but seemingly none the worse for their experience. At least this trick did work on the rats and we had no further trouble.

Although Reg was a building contractor he, like myself, preferred older properties and the freedom of fields. Standing in five acres of farmland, with barns, cowsheds and piggeries stood a lovely old white-washed house surrounded by trees and gardens. Originally it had been Rothley Riding School. It came on the market and it was not long before we purchased the property and moved in.

Some said it was haunted. Apparently a man called Mr Stringer, a scrap iron dealer, had hung himself in the barn. Whilst living there we never had the pleasure of meeting this ghost. On windy nights the shutters would rattle but he never appeared. Eventually we christened him Sebastian. After we had been living there some time something strange did occur. John was awakened from his slumbers with heavy pattering above the ceiling of his bedroom. Naturally we thought he was making up a good story, but he insisted it was real. Then Reg and I also experienced these feet one night, so the next day an investigation took place. Next to the barn had been stacked a pile of bricks for alterations. Rats had found their way on top of these to a hole in the barn and proceeded under the floor boards, climbed up some rafters at the end of the loft, where the house joined the barns over to John's bedroom ceiling and eventually to Reg's and my ceiling. Still no ghost.

Before long we were able to buy our first cow, which we called Grace as it was the day Grace Kelly married Prince Ranier of Monaco. Although hard work was involved, cleaning out pig styes, cowsheds etc. it was so satisfying to have animals again and to be handling new life – lovely little pink piglets, with coats as soft as silk; a dear little calf that could stand almost as soon as it was born and to watch it try to suckle from its mother whilst she turned round to lick it, quietly talking in her way. About three days after giving birth the cow's milk is back to normal. We had a portable milking machine although the eldest son John could milk by hand. After removing the milk we required for the house I would put the remainder in a large bowl and stand it overnight in the cool dairy. In the morning, using a proper skimmer, I skimmed the cream from the top of the milk which was then transferred into a very small churn and made into butter.

Our children and their friends just loved the freedom of the fields. They played football and cricket – the odd ball (fortunately a tennis ball) being lobbed onto the roof of the greenhouse. Cedric had made a canoe whilst at school so this was used on the river which meandered beyond the bottom field. Simba the Samoyed dog was a bit of a nuisance at times. When the children went down to the river he followed as he enjoyed a swim. But at times he would swim up to the canoe and put his paws on it, and of course, the canoe went over, not in a few feet of water but in places at least 10 feet deep. Thankfully the children were all good swimmers. The canoe was stored in what was called the Log Cabin made of old railway sleepers. Sadly one day when the children went down to the fields to get it out it had gone. We never found out who stole it. It was very disheartening for Cedric after all the hard work he had put into making it.

Reg erected a trapeze in the huge barn, also for the children's entertainment. This was an ideal place in case anyone fell, as bales of hay made a soft landing. A hammock was tied to two trees in the first paddock but that soon came to grief. Grace the Guernsey cow was already de-horned when we purchased her, but Sue seemed to have very long horns and it was not long before she went to investigate the hammock, whereupon she delighted in getting her horns so tangled up in it that it had to be removed. After this episode we had Sue de-horned. Quite a simple and apparently painless procedure.

Everything was not always plain sailing. For instance one of the sows gave birth to fifteen piglets, then could not feed them as she had what is called farrowing fever. The vet had to be called to inject her to reduce the fever but this turned out to be catastrophic. While the vet waited with the syringe Mr Webster who was our part time handy man and gardener and I carried a very heavy field gate into the shed to fence off the sow from the piglets. Once it was in position the vet asked us to stand on this gate. I wondered why at the time. The vet clearly expected problems, but none of us were ready for what actually happened. He injected the sow and removed the syringe, but the needle stayed behind. By this time the sow was really fierce and with her snout just lifted the gate, with Mr Webster and myself, completely off the floor. Immediately the vet yelled, "Get that bloody gate out of here and when I shout, open that door for me". It really was funny but very dangerous. The vet grabbed the sow by the tail and whilst she was taking him round in circles he managed to remove the needle. Once again he bellowed to us to open the door and he flew out into the yard.

Once the injection had taken effect the sow settled down, but then came the problem of feeding the fifteen little piglets every two hours. There were losses but Reg and I managed to rear eleven. After a few days they began to feed from a trough. The runt, as the tiny pig is called, was given the name of Little Willie. He was a funny little thing but became very fond of me. As soon as he saw me with a bottle of milk he would sit up on his hind legs and at the same time make a funny noise in what one might call pig language.

The menfolk like to imply that females do not make good farmers. This is entirely wrong, they can look after stock equally as well as the men but what the ladies lack is the indifference to the animals – to be able to sell them without becoming emotional – whereas it is possible for a man to rub his hands together and say aloud, "They should make a good price".

In one respect I was very much like my father when it came to selling some of the animals. In years gone by my father only sealed a deal if he received what is called Luck Money. Whatever he sold he expected to receive a gift of a pound or two. So I soon picked up this trait and believe it or not, it worked. People easily responded. Edgar, my brother, remarked that I was the only member of the family who took after our Dad when doing a deal. In fact this tradition of Luck Money may date back to the Nineteenth Century when Gypsies paid their annual visit to the fair in Horncastle to sell their horses. Right through the ages they have bartered and bargained and with just a clap of the hand from one to the other a sale was sealed.

People from towns and cities are not always aware of what goes on with farm animals. For instance, I had a telephone call from a nurse who was employed by a large firm in Leicester for the sole purpose of attending their staff when necessary. Her residence overlooked our fields and she wanted to know why one of the cows was chasing up and down the fields and "mooing" like mad. She remarked on the fact that she and her husband had moved from the city into the countryside where they could enjoy a more peaceful life.

First of all she was told that the cow was letting it be known that she wanted serving by the bull. But on this occasion we wished to give it a miss. By the next day she would quieten down and return quietly to grazing. The next thing I told the nurse was that if she was expecting peace in the country then she had the wrong area, what with the cock crowing in the early morning, the pigs squealing, the cows mooing, the sheep constantly going baa-baa, calling their own lambs to their side.

If you are near to a Rectory then there is usually a spinney near by where there is a lot of squawking going on when the crows and rooks disagree. Many is the time the doves and pigeons fly into the trees in the gardens and will coo all day long. Then in the Spring the Cuckoo makes his or her appearance to join in the chorus.

To real country lovers all these sounds are "music" to their ears.

At eight weeks old the ten little pigs were sold but not Little Willie. I could not think of selling him until he grew much bigger when it would be out of the question to keep him any longer. As for the ten piglets, they were fine specimens. I set my mind on a price for them. One day a local farmer came to look them over but when I mentioned the price he thanked me for my time and went away. It was not long before the front door bell rang and there he stood cheque book in hand and said, "I really want those pigs and will pay you the asking price".

One Sunday I decided to let out one of the sows into the first paddock. She was due to "pig" any day. She seemed fit and well, and one of the lads had some fun riding on her back. The following day she appeared to be unwell and the vet was sent for. On examination he found she had had a heart attack (not caused by the incident of the day before). A quick decision had to be made. If at all possible we hoped to get her to the abattoir before she died then we would receive some payment but if she died on the journey there it would have been a complete loss. She would have been worth far more had she lived and produced a family whereas £12 was the amount paid in this instance.

The next decision was to sell Sue's calf Bernadene; again this was not easy after having her from birth to a year old. So on the Sunday afternoon in question Reg and John offered to drive her from the field into a shed ready for loading into the cattle truck the next morning. However, she gave them what is commonly called a "run for their money". She took off around the paddock,

Bernadene with Grace

kicking up her hind legs, as much to say, "catch me if you can!". They chased her for a while. In the end John fetched a rope and made a lasso and eventually caught her. But even then she was not giving in so easily: the final scene was the two men hanging on to her almost as if they were part of a rodeo performance. At last she settled down and quietly entered the shed to eat the hay and dairy nuts.

But, alas! she had the last laugh. The next morning, right before our very eyes, there she was happily grazing away back in the field. She had jumped a very high door, the top door having been left open for air and light for her, then over the fence. The cattle truck had to be cancelled until another market day. To entertain another rodeo was certainly not on at that time.

The time came when Little Willie had to go. For years I was teased about being so cruel as to let him go but decisions have to be made however difficult it may be emotionally.

It was not long before the third calamity. In all the time we had kept poultry there was just one night when we failed to drop the slot on the door of the hen house. Next morning when I went to let the hens out and to feed them I was deeply shocked. For as far as I could see there was a trail of feathers and dead hens, a total of 55 down two paddocks towards the river. It was obvious the fox had paid a visit. One thing is for sure: one chicken only was taken to eat, but oh! how they enjoy the killing.

In the first paddock was a huge pile of wood waiting to be sawn up for the fires. Reg decided he would make himself a comfortable position amongst this wood and take his gun and stay out all night until he found the thief. He covered the roof with a tarpaulin, made a cozy seat complete with a cushion and blanket and off he would go on his night duty complete with a flask of coffee and sandwiches.

This went on for four nights. I was convinced he went to sleep. He would brag about his army days and being on guard at night and not sleeping but let's face it, he was a lot younger then. Imagine how we laughed when we were sitting at the table in front of the breakfast room window and who should pass coyly by but the fox which trotted off out of the courtyard and disappeared. Strange too, he was never seen again, so someone had found this culprit. It seems a shame they are such destructive killers as they really are beautiful animals.

At the rear of the house was a cobbled courtyard leading to the stables and barns and garage. To one side stood a lovely old pump with its stone trough below. As the cars had to pass over the well to this pump Reg became worried that after so many years the wooden structure may have deteriorated and that one day it would cave in and one of the cars could get stuck. He decided to investigate. Once the top structure was removed he could see the very fine brickwork of the well which indeed was very deep. If you dropped a pebble in it seemed to take quite a few seconds before you heard the "plop". Reg announced that he wanted all the rubbish around the property to be collected and to be dropped down the well, so it was all hands on deck.

Looking back over the years I regret what happened to a lovely old brass faced grandfather clock. One day Reg came home with this clock which he had purchased from a client for the sum of 7 pounds 10 shillings. At that time I had a great dislike for this kind of clock, so it was put in the loft and one day the children wanted something to play with, so I gave them the clock. The next time I went into the loft I found the children had had a field day and taken it all to pieces, whereupon it too finished up down the well. Eventually the well was sealed and strong concrete lintels put across with final brickwork and cobbles to match the rest of the yard.

As the years have gone by and the lovely old items of furniture and china and bric-a-brac have become part of present day living, there is no wonder I have regretted discarding a beautiful old clock in such a manner that it could never be retrieved to reinstate it to its original glory.

At the side of the stable wall grew an apricot tree which had over the past years produced many pounds of fruit but the following year not one single apricot could be seen. No doubt the roots had been fed from the water in the well and after the rubbish had been thrown down it had soaked up the water.

In the kitchen garden stood an old wooden garden shed which I decided would make a lovely den for all the children. I set about making it very attractive with a table and chairs, curtains at the windows, rugs on the floor and the usual crockery. Everyone was warned about the use of matches but sure enough, after many months of enjoying a refuge of their own one of them brought a candle and some matches.

It seems the candle was burning brightly on the table but they all left the shed and no one thought to blow the candle out. Consequently it set the shed ablaze and the fire engine was sent for. On his way home from collecting the men from a job in Leicester, Reg noticed smoke rising in the distance and said "Somebody is having a good old fire". It was not until he arrived home that he became aware that that "good old fire" was our beautiful old garden shed burnt to the ground.

During the school holidays the boys went train spotting. For the sum of 2/6 they purchased a season ticket and could hop on and off any train at any station. When they arrived home the evening was spent underlining the names of all the trains they had seen that day. Eventually over the years they had seen every engine.

Some days along with their mates they would grab their bicycles and cycle madly down the drive to the main road and down to Rothley Station to see the very famous Master Cutler pass through on its way to Rugby.

In later years John and Cedric had motor cycles and Helen had first a little black Welsh pony called Billy, and then a 16 hands Chestnut which she called Paddy. They looked a strange pair side by side, like Little and Large. Paddy would suddenly set off down the field with little Billy trekking behind. One day Billy took Paddy by storm, looked up at him as much as to say, "Just you watch this" then took off. He just flew down the field. Paddy was too amazed to even try to catch him.

John has always been more dedicated and would spend more time on his studies than his brother Cedric.

Paddy and Billy being ridden by Helen and her friend Carole

In a way he has followed in his father's footsteps. He has worked long hours, with that strong determination to withstand the many pitfalls that occur in business until he reached his ambition of being successful.

He, along with his friend Roger, would attend the lectures of the St. John's Ambulance every Friday evening. These were held at the Rothley Temple, now a hotel known as *Rothley Court*. It was here that John met Jennifer, and after a while brought her home. It was then that we realised he was very attracted to her. Soon there were wedding bells. Their home was created by Reg. He converted the cowshed, store sheds and piggeries into a lovely bungalow for them.

The day of the wedding arrived, guests were coming and going, but I kept my eye on the clocks. For years they were always set to be ten minutes fast. But lo and behold! when Reg and I arrived at the Church I could not believe my eyes. Jennifer was alighting from the bride's car.

I turned to Reg and said, "Our clocks are always ten minutes fast, we are not late." It was then that he informed me that he had put the clocks to the correct time the night previously, so no wonder we only just made it. We just managed to settle in our seats before Jennifer walked down the aisle on the arm of her father.

The following year our grandson was born and christened Mark, and three years later Nicholas was born.

seven
MOVE TO BLABY

*E*ventually Reg and Tim took early retirement and we bought a beautiful old house down a very long lane in a village called Blaby. John being now married, just Cedric and Helen went along with us to our new home. At first we renovated the bungalow which was sold with the property, and let this to two very nice men. Then the very old part of the house Reg made into flats.

Helen attended the Teachers Training College at Scraptoft, travelling daily in her own car, whilst Cedric was with a firm of accountants trading under the name of Hosiery Federation and was sent out to firms to check the books.

One evening as he journeyed home he caught sight of a Sunbeam Talbot car for sale in a garage about two miles from Blaby. Eventually he called in and arranged to purchase this car offering his own little sports car in part exchange. The deal took place on a Saturday. Apparently this garage was owned by two partners, one a Cypriot and the other Turkish. The Cypriot was due back from his honeymoon on this same Saturday. However we were unaware that Nazme the Turk should not have sold the car in the absence of the Cypriot. After a night out with his friends, Cedric parked his new car in the courtyard and went to bed. Strange though it might seem, the next morning he told us that he had had a dream that his Sunbeam was being driven down the drive. In fact it was no dream, it was true. The Cypriot, back from his honeymoon, waited until the early hours of the Sunday morning and fetched the Sunbeam and took it back to the garage. A fierce battle took place between the Cypriot and the Turk.

At about seven o'clock that Sunday morning the front door bell rang and there stood Nazme the Turk informing us of the incident that had taken place. Reg and Cedric went off to the garage along with Nazme who then gave them the keys and they brought the Sunbeam back home. The Cypriot had meanwhile gone home to bed.

Lo! and behold at 2 o'clock on the Sunday afternoon a big lorry and crane were seen coming up the drive, driven by the Cypriot. Without permission he drove straight into the courtyard and several men tumbled out of the lorry. Then up came a mini van and out came more men. We immediately telephoned the

Police. It was just like a scene from a movie. Reg, Nazme and myself stood to protect the Sunbeam. One man grabbed Nazme and almost knocked him unconscious. Our friends took care of him whilst Reg and I ran down the drive picking up timber and all kinds of things to put in the drive to hold up these men from leaving the property until the Police arrived. One fellow picked up a very large coke bucket and threw it at me just missing my face by about an inch. This force of men was too much for us. They soon cleared the drive and off they went. Nazme was so badly hurt that Reg took him to hospital and even as they went down the lane the Police were nowhere to be seen. By the time the Police had arrived all was over.

When they eventually arrived they took down all the particulars and at a later date the Cypriot and his men were taken to court by the Police and finished up being fined heavily.

However, before the Sunbeam was returned we had to wait many months for our civil court case to be heard. By that time the car had stood out during a bad winter, water left in the radiator and so on. We won the case but the Cypriot had engaged a wonderful barrister and at one time I thought we would lose the case against him. In fact we finished up as losers, the Sunbeam was now not worth the original price. Cedric had to use our car for many months which cost him more in petrol. In this case the innocent suffered and not the guilty.

Once life was back to normal Reg and I decided to turn the barns into showrooms for antiques – he to do the repairs to the furniture and me to take over the selling of them. This became a very interesting hobby. Along the way we met many interesting people, doctors, solicitors, manufacturers, butchers and not forgetting the man and his wife who were buying their first home and preferring old furniture.

I purchased in a junk shop a model of Ann Hathaway's Cottage for 10 shillings, on the base of which was marked the price of 7/6. A dealer came and offered me £25 for it, and of course I let it go – this was indeed a wonderful profit.

Reg and I would travel into Lincolnshire at weekends and stay overnight at the Golf Hotel at Woodhall Spa, going around all the antique shops during the day to make further purchases.

On one occasion we had purchased quite a big load from our favourite dealer in Grantham, including a heavy stone mill wheel. It was Autumn and the nights were getting darker and cooler. We left Grantham at about 8 o'clock in the evening and as we climbed a steep hill there was a sound like a clap of thunder.

The trailer had gone careering across the road and into a hedge. There was not a piece of furniture to be seen, just the mill wheel still in the trailer. We needed help and decided that one of us must cadge a lift from a passing motorist whilst the other went back to Grantham to seek out the dealer.

I did not fancy staying with the car on this dark lonely road so volunteered to go for help. There were no cars in sight for half an hour, until a motorcycle appeared. Reg flagged him down and soon I was riding pillion behind this motor cyclist and really enjoying flying through the air.

It was not until I came "back to earth" that I considered the risks in a five mile motorcycle ride behind a strange man. In fact he was an extremely nice fellow. I took him into the pub where I knew at this time of night I would find the dealer and his brother, and treated him to a drink. Jim and Tom the two dealers guessed that there was something wrong when they saw me enter the pub.

Soon we were heading back to the scene of the disaster to retrieve the furniture, which had flown over a very high hedge. It seemed unbelievable that it was undamaged. The dealers decided it would be best for them to take the mill wheel back to the warehouse in their van. All the furniture was put safely onto the trailer, and had just been securely tied down when a Police car appeared. The only other motorist to have passed during the operation of re-loading the trailer had warned the Police that there were thieves about. Fortunately, Jim knew the Sergeant and just calmly said, "Hi Sarge, we followed our friends and wanted to make sure they negotiated the hill okay before we returned to Grantham. We have just re-tied the load". All was well and we travelled safely back to Blaby.

It was not long before Christmas was approaching and the local Lay Preacher of the Baptist Church paid us a visit. He required a donkey for the festivities and had heard that we had one. As Dusty, the mother, had not long produced her foal Lulu, I was in doubt as to lending her unaccompaied, in case she became obstinate, so I offered my services and we made the necessary arrangements for a certain evening. I walked down the lane at least half a mile with Dusty and reported to the Baptist Chapel. Everyone was awaiting my arrival and soon I was bedecked in a flowing robe, a sash around my waist and a checked tea towel draped around my head. A little girl was chosen to sit on Dusty to be Mary and a little lad walked at the side as Joseph. Off we went down every street singing carols as we went along making a collection. At last we reached the precinct, the main shopping centre, and sang more carols. Dusty was an absolute angel and stood perfectly still the whole time.

Eventually we headed back to the Chapel. The Lay Preacher asked me if I would take Dusty inside. This looked totally out of the question because there were four stone steps to climb to gain entrance to the Chapel. But Dusty climbed the steps and went down to the altar where someone had placed some hay for her. Yet again she stood quietly munching away at the hay, oblivious to the lights and the singing.

After the service I headed for home. As Dusty and I started on our journey it began to snow. It was a lovely evening and I felt so happy. However, I had not thought to remove the long robes and tea towel. Soon a car came along and the occupant called to me. A man got out and approached me, saying that he could not believe his eyes, seeing someone in Eastern dress leading a donkey, with the snow falling, it was incredible. The only thing that was out of place was the red rear light on the donkey's tail, otherwise it looked like a scene from a Christmas Card. When I spoke he recognised me, as he kept poultry down the lane. Later that evening the front door bell rang and who should be standing there but the preacher and his wife with a most beautiful bouquet for me. This completed a most wonderful evening.

The donkeys were really purchased for the two grandchildren but unfortunately they were not in the least bit interested, so really it was a waste of time feeding them and cleaning them out. It was not an easy decision to part with them, especially the little foal Lulu, but we sold them to a good home.

Somehow, along the grapevine, the Vet's secretary heard that we had two vacant paddocks so asked if she could bring her lovely chestnut horse called Kerry to occupy them. Whilst in the previous field she rented, soon after the horse was gelded, some boys chased him into a ditch of dirty water and he remained there all night long, causing him serious suffering.

He had been with us several weeks when, one saturday afternoon, I saw him lying on the grass in a most distressing way. Even from the bedroom window I could see he was dead. The Vet was sent for immediately and the news broken to the owner. The post mortem proved that he had eaten a tiny piece of Yew tree which of course is a killer to horses and beasts. The Yew hedge had been there years and was never touched by previous horses, but Kerry must have stretched over the fence and managed to nibble just a sprig. I cried and was so amazed that the owner never shed a tear and was more concerned about getting insurance money for the loss. Soon men came from the abattoir and removed Kerry's body. After this ordeal it was decided not to let the paddocks any more.

Radio Leicester was initially one of the first local stations to open on November 8th in the year 1967. That very afternoon the telephone rang. Helen answered the call and turned to me and said, "It is for you Mother". I asked who it was and Helen said that she didn't know, fully aware what was to come and put me right on the spot. When I picked up the telephone a voice said, "This is Radio Leicester, our first day on the air. We have tried many numbers but so far without success. What we are hoping for is to encourage members of the public to sing, say or recite something, will you do something for us to get us started?" I was somewhat "Taken by storm" At first I tried to avoid the issue but they pleaded with me to have a bash.

On the spur of the moment there was only one thing I could think of which I used to sing to the children and grandchildren and I pointed out that it was perhaps a little stupid. But the voice over the air persisted. Eventually I said, "Well here goes, you have asked for it so here it is.

> *Get upon a puff puff*
> *Early in the morning*
> *See them on the platform*
> *All in a row*
> *Man on the engine*
> *Blows his little whistle* (whereupon I whistled)
> *Chuff, chuff, chuff and away we go.*

Oh! yes the voice was very polite and thanked me. But for weeks I had to endure a lot of teasing. One wonders what the reaction was at the other end of the telephone. At least I tried.

When Cedric was young he seemed to be accident prone. First of all he was knocked down by a car when crossing the road near to our home. The men from our building firm were doing a job next door using a concrete mixer. Cedric was aware of this and asked his father if he could go to them and watch them to which his father agreed. I, for one, was not in favour of this but his father said he would be looked after by the men. Alas! he suddenly left them and ran across the road and was knocked down. Fortunately he was not seriously hurt.

The second occasion was when he fell out of the lorry his father was driving. Again he survived without injury.

On the third, and last time, he was not so lucky. He and his brother, John, were playing cowboys and Indians, using their bows and home-made arrows out of the dried stalks of Michaelmas daisies when John fired an arrow and caught Cedric in the eye. He came rushing into the house blood pouring down his face. Immediately Reg and I took him to hospital. For a month we had many anxious hours but at last the bandage was removed from his eye and all was well. Oh! what a relief.

When Cedric celebrated his 21st Birthday we were living at Blaby. To accommodate all his friends on this occasion we decided to paint and decorate the very large barn. We had the chance to buy a very large old mahogany sideboard which made a super bar. Festoons and paper flowers adorned the walls. The buffet was served in one of the garages nearby, this too had had a coat of paint and was even adorned with bunting. When I cooked the eighteen chickens it reminded me of my mother cooking as many in preparation for my wedding in 1941. Everyone thoroughly enjoyed themselves in spite of dancing being a little more difficult on a concrete floor. In fact we tried hard to improve it and I even shredded candle wax all over and rubbed it in. At around 2 a.m. all the guests had departed, or so we thought, when suddenly Cedric entered the house holding the hand of a very attractive blonde called Lynda.

Slowly this friendship blossomed and eventually they became man and wife. For a time they lived with us whilst Reg converted two old cottages into one dwelling in the delightful village of Cossington. On one of Cedric's visits to Lynda's parents home his car broke down right in the middle of Leicester. As he clambered out of the vehicle a policeman approached him and began to question him. There was no wonder really. In fact Cedric was on his way to a Tramps Supper dressed in my old tatty Harris Tweed coat, torn trousers, raggy mittens on his hands, an old trilby hat on his head and to complete the outfit a sooty face. At that time he owned a lovely sports car and to be dressed like this was enough to make any policeman suspicious.

Both John and Cedric decided to choose accountancy as a profession and worked for the same firm for a number of years then went their separate ways. Cedric now has his own business with the continual struggle and long hours.

Meanwhile Lynda gave birth to a lovely little girl whom they christened Charlotte. She was so tiny when she was born, but how lovely to hold a beautiful little granddaughter. Within a year James Rupert was born. He was quite a contrast to his little sister. Both children are now at school and Charlotte is very artistic.

Then tragedy struck which affected the whole family. Lynda's health began to deteriorate. Eventually she was sent to a neuro-surgeon at the Queen's Medical Centre, Nottingham. He diagnosed the presence of an *acoustic neuroma*, which is a tumour of the inner ear. This necessitated a life-saving operation on the tumour. Already the size of an egg, it had the potential to increase to far larger proportions, with devastating consequences. After a long and complicated operation in 1987, at the Queens Medical Centre, and with further convalescence, Lynda made a remarkable recovery.

Whilst at Blaby Reg purchased two peacocks which were named Bill and Ben. As you approached the house there stood a huge sycamore tree. Each evening these two birds hopped from branch to branch until they reached the top and then settled down for the night. They were also joined by a pheasant who took a fancy to them. But in the morning it was amazing to see them fly down without catching any of the branches.

On calling to them from the kitchen window they would fan out their beautiful plumage and do a kind of dance then tuck in to a feed of glacé cherries. We had hoped to enjoy having Bill and Ben around the property but they became a real headache. They would fly off and not return. We would have to get the car out and go and hunt for them. At times they returned and always to the kitchen window for food. On one occasion we appealed to the public in the evening paper, the Leicester Mercury, to kindly inform us if they were sighted. The heading in the paper was, "Has anyone seen Bill and Ben the peacocks?"

Sadly we found one of them lying on a disused railway line having been shot. So we gave the other one to someone who kept peacocks. It seems that these two peacocks would not have strayed away if they had had a lady friend, a fact of which we had not been aware at the time.

Holidays were usually spent with John and Jennifer, Elizabeth her sister, and her mother Kitty and father Frank, either in Wales or Cornwall.

On one occasion John took his little motor boat out to sea, as he was mad keen on fishing. John persuaded Frank and Reg to go with him. He knew what the ladies saw as they sat on the beach was three men, each wearing a straw hat, setting off to sea in this small boat. They had been gone about an hour when we became aware that some distance along the beach, men were busy taking out a life line, and a Land Rover drove to the water's edge. By this time we were aware that somewhere out at sea someone had signalled for help. Even then we never gave it a thought that it would be our men folk. It seems that John had shut the engine off whilst they were fishing, but when they wanted to return to the beach it would not start again. At this moment a ship passed very near and the lashing of the waves upset the boat.

John and Frank could swim. Reg on the other hand could not, and at one stage was trapped under the boat. He had a very lucky escape as the boat struck him on his ribs and he was bruised for many days. At last they arrived safely back to shore. To some degree they appeared to have enjoyed their escapade and this made conversation for many months afterwards.

eight
FINLAND & BEYOND

*I*n January 1973 Helen was appointed as the Eng-
lish Teacher in a Kindergarten known as the
English Club of Hamina some forty miles West of the
Russian Border. She had an assistant named Pirjo and so
Helen taught her English and she taught Helen Finnish.

At first Helen lived with a Finnish family, no flats
being available at that time. During her summer break she travelled from
Hamina to Austria, where Reg and I met up with her for two weeks holiday.

Once back in England Reg started work on making a folding bed and table
and stools. A flat had become available for Helen and as furniture was so
expensive in Finland she decided that on her return to Hamina she would take
her car, and take as much furniture and effects with her as possible. Eventually
the Renault was packed to capacity leaving just enough room for the driver.

I went with Cedric and his wife Lynda as the advance party on the journey
to Felixstowe followed by Helen. On reaching the quayside her car was put
aboard the Finnish vessel. Apparently she was the only passenger. This
arrangement had previously been made on Helen's behalf by the Governors of
the Kindergarten in Hamina, who were friends of the Captain. He graciously
invited us up to Helen's cabin and ordered drinks to be served.

At last the boat was made ready to sail and Helen stayed on the top deck
waving to us until she went out of sight. She came home for Christmas, our dog
Shandy a lovely golden retriever went absolutely crazy once she walked in
through the door.

Reg and I promised Helen that we would think of visiting her. In July 1974
we left England on our first visit to Finland, landing at Helsinki airport where
we were met by Helen who had driven her banana yellow Renault from Hamina.

Our first night was spent in the Hotel Dipoli part of the University of Helsinki
which was used for student accommodation. Saturday was spent in Helsinki
looking around the historical buildings, the open market by the harbour, and
lastly in the main shop of Stockman which is like Harrods in London.

On the Sunday we travelled to the railway station. Helen first of all settled
us at a table in the restaurant and ordered drinks, then she set off to put the car

on the train to Lapland. Meanwhile we were joined by a Finnish gentleman. He saw Reg's cigarettes which were Players so he took out his Finnish ones and although they could not understand each others language they finished up by exchanging the cigarettes. Then we boarded the train and were shown to our compartment where there were four bunks booked for our journey. After having a meal in the train's dining car we returned to our compartment. Helen chose the top bunk and Reg and I the bottom ones. This was a through train to Lapland and we were not due to alight until 8 o'clock the next morning. Our journey took us due North direct to Rovaniemi, which is the capital of Finnish Lapland within the Arctic Circle. The views as we travelled were magnificent. It is well known for being the land of the midnight sun and Northern Lights, the Aurora Borealis. The sky was ablaze almost as if it was on fire which shone down onto the lakes causing a mind blowing effect with the background of tall fir trees.

I had intended the roll call to be at 6 a.m. instead of which somehow I misjudged the time on my watch and woke Reg and Helen at 5 a.m. Reg had a shave and it was not until sometime later that we realised it was not yet 6 o'clock. Believe me I was most unpopular and it seemed an eternity waiting until the train stopped at 8 o'clock.

Helen collected the car from the train and we made our way to Rukatuntari and booked in to a hotel. Later on we travelled some distance to enjoy the scenery but on the journey back to the hotel as we climbed a very steep hill the suspension went on the car. That evening the chair lifts were not working owing to a storm so we started to walk downhill to find the garage where we had purchased petrol some time before. They were very efficient – they telephoned for a new part which had to be flown from Europe to Helsinki then on to Lapland. Meanwhile the car had been towed to the garage. A car was put at our disposal and we were driven back to the hotel.

After we had dined and wined, a Finnish gentleman made his way to our table and I was quite shocked when he bowed to me and not to Helen. Then he turned to Reg and asked his permission for me to dance with him, still in Finnish which Helen translated. It appears that this procedure is a tradition of the Finnish people.

We danced well together and when the music stopped he spoke to me using his hands to express that he was a fisherman. Like the English he too exaggerated the length of the fish by at least 30 inches. To save the day the music started and we glided off once more. After this dance he escorted me back to our table and bowed to Reg and Helen and took his leave. I felt very honoured in spite of my age, at that time being 56 years.

Within 24 hours the car was brought to the hotel and we packed our bags and commenced the next part of the journey further North where we saw Lake Imira. We visited the oldest wooden church in Lapland, Sodambyllöä. Every grave had a candle burning brightly under a glass dome. We then proceeded

South (still in Lapland) to Kuusamo where again accommodation had been booked by Helen at a hotel. That evening we partook of Reindeer steaks for the first time in our lives, but I especially enjoyed the sweet Arctic Cloudberries which look like peachy coloured raspberries.

While we ate our dinner the view from the window of the dining room was of a huge lake and men riding the pine logs. The next day we started our journey back to Hamina, our next stop being South Kuopio where we stopped off at a race meeting of Horse Trotting with the two wheeled carriages. I placed one or two bets but this was not my lucky day. Here it was very noticeable that many of the teams were owned by the Hungarian Gypsies.

For dinner that evening we tasted a very special fish pie called Kalakukko made of fish, potatoes and pork in pastry. Immediately we had finished our meal an Englishman came across to our table, insisted on buying us drinks and took Helen off to dance. He taught English in the University in Kuopia and invited us to visit the University the next morning and to have coffee with him. He had a degree in Oriental languages but he felt that Finnish was more difficult to learn.

After taking our leave we travelled South East to Imatra. Here we saw the water falls and the Sentry Posts on the Russian border. Before leaving for Hamina we travelled by boat near to the Russian border towards Karelicu, originally the centre of Finland's cultural tradition and economy. Sibelius the Finnish composer wrote the music of the Karelia Suite which epitomises the culture and landscape of this East Finnish area now claimed by Russia.

Then our final journey South West took us back to Hamina. Here we spent time in the market place and shops buying presents to take back to England.

One outstanding feature was the statue of Varvara, an old Finnish lady who took Finnish bread to the troops in a wheel barrow during the Winter War when Russia invaded Finland on November 30th 1939. By March 12th 1940 they had conquered a large area of Finland's Eastern frontiers.

Dorothy, Helen and Eric with
Varvara

Another feature was a huge mill wheel called the kissing stone, where you had to kiss from each side through the large hole in the centre.

Hamina is an unusual town built on a circular plan almost like a spider's web. In the centre is the town hall and streets go off in all directions.

Six kilometres away we came to a lovely sandy beach called Long Beach Pitkäränta. Our last night was spent at the Hamina Sailing Club. At the harbour we pressed a button which rang a bell in the Club, whereupon a boat was rowed over to pick us up and take us over to the Club. Here we met the Commodore and his Tapio and Helena who were friends of Helen. Next morning we had to get up at 3 a.m. to make our journey to the airport at Helsinki and return to England.

Once we arrived back in England Reg complained of headaches. This was most unusual as he really enjoyed good health apart from an odd cold or two. He looked very pale and slowly his appetite lessened. All this concerned me so I telephoned the doctor to make an appointment. When Reg returned home after his visit he made little comment other than he was to see a specialist within the next few days.

The appointment was made and I accompanied Reg to a private address in Leicester. When he came out of the consulting room he appeared his usual self. I offered to drive home but Reg said that he was okay and away we went, but his driving was so erratic that I realised that something was wrong. On reaching home he said he had something wrong with his stomach and had to have an operation. Still I was not satisfied. I felt that there was something more serious that he was not telling me, so when Helen came home in the evening I asked her to talk with the specialist over the phone. He immediately told her "I knew that your father would not tell your mother the truth as he loves her too much to inform her of the real truth. Sadly he has cancer and an operation is imperative". In the November Reg went into hospital and was operated on. That evening my two sons, Helen and I all visited him. The sister spoke to me and said that the specialist wished to see me in his office. I went with Helen. The specialist was indeed very kind but we were both devastated when he informed us that it was an inoperable cancer and that he had at the most four months to live. The specialist apologised for having to give us such awful news and said we were to remain in his office for as long as we wished before returning to the ward.

I can find no words to express the shock we both felt, yet we had to be brave and calm and collected and return to the ward to Reg's bedside where stood the two boys. We acted quite normally which gave John and Cedric the idea that all was well. It was not until we left Reg and walked along the corridor that we broke the sad news.

For Reg's sake we had to be very brave and visited him regularly. Eventually he was sent to a convalescent home nearby but he was most unhappy there so I took it upon myself to request that I nurse him and would like to take him home. I had to consult the Registrar and after signing certain documents saying that I would accept responsibility Reg came home to Blaby.

Once home, he requested a bed downstairs preferably in the larger of the two lounges. He had good and bad days, read a lot and enjoyed the TV. Cricket

Shandy

the cat and Shandy the dog spent a lot of time with him. In fact, Shandy always waited for me to bring in a bowl of water and towels ready for the morning blanket bath and then he nestled down near to the bed. It seemed almost an every day ritual to him.

When Shandy was a puppy we had taught him to respond to the words, "Go to Mummy" and, "Go to Daddy", when we were partaking of our coffee and biscuits before retiring to bed. Consequently, when Reg collapsed one day in the cloakroom he called to Shandy to "Go fetch Mummy". Shandy shot upstairs but came straight down again. Reg was aware that he was not coming to me but on the third attempt he came upstairs and barked incessantly to which I responded and followed him downstairs to where Reg lay on the floor. The St. Bernard dog has always been noted for the saving of lives but it is apparent that any dog with some form of training answers the call of distress.

That Christmas all the family sat down to Christmas Dinner. Reg managed to get to the table in his wheel chair. We all put on a brave face, although we were aware that this could be our last Christmas as a family. His birthday was on the 14th of January and he was still eating fairly well and enjoying his visitors and an odd game of cards. He loved to play Solo.

Spring was not far away. First of all the Blackthorn appeared in the paddock with its radiance of lovely white blossom. Then the pretty pale green of willow trees standing upright in the pond. In fact Spring was really early that year almost as if it was for the benefit of Reg to see and behold before he departed to another world. Soon the Crocus appeared under the huge Sycamore tree with their lovely shades of yellow, white and purple hues, so I put Reg into his wheel chair, wrapped him up well and pushed him round the garden.

On the way back to the house he asked to get out of his wheel chair and with an immense effort made it through the door to his beloved workshop where he had spent so many hours creating with his hands and machinery the many different works of art from the woods of oak, mahogany, pine and walnut. It was very sad to see him. One wonders as he looked at his bench and his tools, his planer, machine saw and wood-turning lathe if he knew in his own heart that he would never use them again.

Eventually this proved too much for him as he really was so very weak and he almost collapsed as he struggled towards his wheel chair.

During our many years together he had always bought flowers for me and in spite of being so ill he continued to have flowers brought to the house for me each week.

Strange, though the specialist had warned us of the short time Reg had left to spend with us each morning as I drew back the curtains somehow I felt rewarded as here was the dawn and he was still with us. At times like this one looks to "one above" and thanks him for your husband's life being spared for yet another day.

On the Monday prior to his passing away on the Thursday I was convinced that Reg realised that he was getting weaker and he asked me straight out, "Am I going to die? I want you to tell me the truth. Please hold my hands and tell me." This was the most heart rending thing I had ever done in my life. There are no words to convey the grief and anguish you feel when you are faced with telling the man you love that he is going to die. I had no choice but to tell him the awful truth. I could not hold back the tears. Reg held me tightly to his body. He was so strong and brave giving me the strength to carry on.

We talked for a long time. He thanked me for being a good wife and mother and said that as I was still young if ever I should marry again I had his blessing. This indeed proved the kind of generous man he had always been. He also said, "I have asked the two boys to always look after their mother and I have provided for you whereby you will not want for anything". In the past he had helped the two boys and even at the last he thought of Helen and said to me, "I shall not be able to do anything for Helen so if you can afford it will you help her?"

During his illness my friend Eileen was of great help and comfort and so too was her son Nigel. His father had died when he was quite young and so he had become very attached to Reg. He came to see Reg every day and mourned greatly when he passed away.

Another of the boys, now a grown man, named Martin visited him every Sunday morning. He wanted to show his appreciation for the many happy hours he had shared with the other children during our life at the Paddocks so many years before.

On March 13th 1975 Reg passed peacefully away in the way in which he would have wished and that was with great dignity. His last words to me were the words of the song, "Walk on, walk on with hope in your heart and you'll never walk alone". To hear this song today brings tears to my eyes.

He belonged to a prominent family in the district, a number of homes in the immediate locality exist as a reminder of the extensive building operations of the family business.

Originally a carpenter of exceptional skill, he gladly put his services at the disposal of others in need. He could always be counted upon to cope immediately with practical problems, no matter at how inconvenient an hour they might arise.

He was a man of wide interests. During the latter part of his life he showed the versatility of his professional skills – using them this time, not to create something new, but to recreate what is antique, so that it might continue to be a thing of beauty and usefulness. In his younger days he played cricket for both Rothley and Newtown Linford. Whenever I attended these matches he was generally bowled out for a duck. Seems he might have tried to show off a little in my presence.

The day of the funeral came and his ashes were put into an oak casket that he had made himself and so he was laid to rest in the Churchyard at Swithland where once he was a Warden in the Church and where his sons John and Cedric and his daughter Helen attended Sunday School.

After Grandpa Simmons passed away John and Jennifer decided to tell Mark. Nicholas was too young to understand. On their next visit after the funeral Mark stepped out of the car, ran towards me and holding my hand said to me, "I do love you Nannie Simmons". Almost as if he was saying, "Now that Grandpa has gone I will look after you". It took great willpower not to break down at these loving words.

Swithland retains a wealth of history, of the quarries in which the notable slate was worked and the old stone cottages which recall the heyday of the industry. This slate of a dark blue hue covered the roofs of many of the older buildings in the County of Leicestershire. It also furnished many of the fine tombstones on which generations of the local carvers lavished their art.

The Church enshrines many ancient memorials, the oldest being a brass finely mounted on a wall, bearing the figure of a 15th Century nun named Agnes Scott who is believed to have lived in a cave near to Leicester called Black Agnes Bower. Amongst the most touching tablets are those of two sons of the 6th earl of Lanesborough, Francis Butler and his brother Brian who fell in the First World War.

The most curious monument is the elaborate 18th Century tomb of Sir John Danvers. On two sides are engravings on Swithland slate, one of a ship in sail and of a church below a hill with the couplet as follows:

When young I sailed to India, East and West
But aged in this port must lye at rest

Another scene of ploughing has these lines:

Be cheerful Ol Man! a labour to live
The merciful God a blessing will give.

It is said that Sir John Danvers could not be buried entirely within the Churchyard as he did not wish to be parted from his beloved dog and so it was that his tomb was built into the wall whereby the faithful animal could be near to his master in unconsecrated ground. His own appearance was likened to that of the Knave of Spades. One person who remembered him well left the following picture of him: *He was remarkably fond, like the Chinese, of painting everything red, so much so that every door, window shutter and gatepost in the towns of Swithland and Mountsorrel was so decorated.*

This part of Leicestershire is rich in reservoirs and many water fowl flock to them. There are mallards, coots and great-crested grebes. The golden eye is a frequent visitor, flying South from its breeding quarters in northern and eastern Europe. The drakes of this species are a striking sight with their black and white plumage, their heads are dark bottle green and white check patches below the golden eye which gives these birds their name. As with most members of the duck family, the females are of a duller brownish colour. During the last century all these handsome birds were almost exterminated due to the feathers being in great demand for the decoration of women's hats.

On a hill in the park stands Swithland Hall ancestral home of the Earls of Lanesborough.

The year 1993 marked the 66th year of the special Blue Bell Service of Thanksgiving in Swithland Woods, one of Leicestershire's beauty spots. People from all the villages attend this service. It really is a most outstanding sight with the carpet of blue bells.

Blue Bells you carpet all the woods
Every time the Spring's returning
There now just see them gaily nod
As they reveal their secret

Then once more the birds begin to sing
Spring and sunshine wakens everything
Then Blue Bells appear
To welcome Fairy Spring

After the funeral I had the flu which left me with a nasty cough. The doctor suggested to Helen that a holiday would be my best cure, especially as I had been on day and night duty for the last four months and rest was most necessary. Hence at the end of April we went to Greece. It is strange how some people get the wrong idea about another person or persons. Naturally they thought mother and daughter were looking out to catch a man, until they were informed to the contrary.

Before we left these shores Helen and I went into Leicester to do some shopping and happened to pass the wig counter in one of the stores. She suggested I tried a wig on as one's hair can be such a nuisance on holiday. Well I chose a most suitable one but it amazed me when Helen also purchased hers, as she had lovely long hair. We boarded the plane both in our wigs. But each evening Helen would remove her wig and go down to dinner with long hair. Everyone would stare but never said anything.

On the last evening before our return to England I suggested that if the friends we had met on this holiday were in agreement I would request that a table could be laid for dinner to accommodate all of us. Also I ordered champagne and a special sweet to be served. As the waiter approached the table to serve the first course a false tooth fell from his mouth, hit the table and bounced back to him. Fortunately he caught it. This caused great laughter. He was full of apologies. Apparently he had been to the dentist that day and the tooth in question was a temporary measure.

I had no choice, like any widow, but to come to terms with living alone and starting a new life. In September that year Helen returned to Finland promising to be with me at Christmas. At the beginning of December Helen telephoned me to announce that she had booked a skiing holiday for me, herself and two friends, Kenneth and Valerie near the Italian border. This was a great relief as I was not looking forward to my first Christmas without Reg.

We should have flown from Heathrow at 2 p.m. on the 23rd December but the fog was so dense that we were transported by coach to Stansted where we eventually boarded the plane at midnight.

The plane had to land at Verona Airport because of this delay, meaning our journey took about three days by coach up into the mountains to our hotel.

The following evening we threw open the doors of the balcony from the bedroom and what a wonderful sight to behold, the tall fir trees with fairy lights shimmering in the distance as the snow began to fall, with the bells tolling out their Christmas welcome.

The following day the four of us set out to hire the necessary gear. Helen and her two friends could ski so off they would go up the mountains until lunch time. Meanwhile I joined a learners' class and was the eldest of the group.

It was easy climbing the slopes, but the fun started as we all attempted our first skiing lesson. Our instructor could not speak a word of English so we just hoped we were doing the right thing at the right time. When it came to my turn to ski down the slope the Instructor called out the usual word which sounded like Hoopsla. At least I gave the other members of the group something to laugh about. As I set off each day on my run, firstly my knitted hat fell off, then down I went. The instructor retrieved my hat and put it on my head then had to help me to get up on to my skis once more. I usually made it down to the bottom without further mishaps. One young man came back to England with a broken leg. I thanked my lucky stars that I remained in once piece.

In the evenings we would sit at a long table and eat our meal. We were joined by two more married couples and a man on his own. During the meal we conversed and it was most unusual to find that the man who was alone was a Head Master, the two couples were also teachers, Val and Ken and Helen were teachers too. I was the only outsider. But the husband of one of the teachers who sat next to me suddenly looked at me and said what lovely lips I had. That really made my day, or rather evening.

Once the skiing holiday was over I had to get down to seriously thinking of moving house. Although I did not wish to leave this beautiful Victorian House it was far too big, and very isolated being surrounded by 86 acres of farm land.

Eventually the house and grounds were sold. I also owned a seven acre field and when it came to the sale of this I found out that the original tenant had vacated it and another one had illegally moved his cattle into the field. He was a stubborn old farmer and flatly refused to remove his animals. As a joke I said to him that if he did not remove his animals I would leave the gate open and let them out.

Several days later I received a telephone call at 6 a.m. saying that the gate was open and the animals were heading for the main road. I immediately telephoned the Wigston Police and explained the situation, including the threat of leaving the gate open, and that it had really happened. Eventually it was found that this man had hoped to get me into trouble with the Police, but instead things did not go the way he intended and I soon had a vacant field for sale. On the following Sunday afternoon a farmer came to the house to make an offer for this land. It was a lovely sunshiny afternoon and I invited him to sit on the seat in the garden whilst I went indoors to make a cup of tea. As we sat talking and drinking I suddenly asked this farmer his name. I could not believe my ears when I heard him say "Mr Piggin". It took a lot of restraint not to laugh in his face.

I watched the properties for sale in the local papers and came across the advertisement for an old farm house in Newtown Linford. Although it was in need of refurbishment this did not deter me from making an offer for it. When I told my two sons I intended buying it they thought at first that I was crazy. To me this was a big challenge and something I needed to recover from the loss of Reg.

When Reg was in business as a builder he taught me a lot, and I put all this to good use. Apparently this property had once belonged to the Grey Family, none other than Lady Jane Grey the Nine Days Queen. My name, under the then surname of Simmons, was recorded in a book published on the History of Newtown Linford.

The village is the doorstep to Bradgate Park, one of Leicestershire's loveliest beauty spots. It is a charming hamlet with thatched and timbered dwellings and a Medieval Church in a peaceful setting by the stream.

First of all the two pitched roofs had to be re-roofed. All the old Swithland slates had to be removed and sorted and a further supply of slates purchased to complete the job. The lead had to be renewed between the two pitches, water had already made its way down the inner walls of the property. During this time I had had a good offer for the house at Blaby on condition the purchaser could have possession within one month. It was too good an opportunity to refuse, so I set about clearing a huge stone-built barn ready for occupation whilst work continued on the house.

The walls were washed down by hose, the floor concreted, the farm dairy made into a kitchen with a bath in one corner and electricity installed.

Moving day came. All the furniture was stored down both sides of the barn and down the middle leaving walking space each side. Pictures, brass plaques and anything that could be hung up was fixed to the walls. My bed had a canopy fixed over the top to prevent any dust or cobwebs falling down on me when I was asleep.

Helen's bedroom was the granary over the kitchen and to reach this one had to climb a rough sort of open stairs. Her friend Pirjo came from Finland to stay and she too slept up there with Helen.

One Saturday evening as they returned from a visit to another friend in Nottingham they came in and were very noisy and woke me, and I yelled "Can you at least make less noise and not set the whole barn alight?" Nevertheless on going up the loft stairs to bed one of them let out a shriek. It was not until the next morning that I found out why. In the dustpan outside the door was a dead rat, no doubt carried up there by one of the cats.

October came and still the alterations were not complete. The evenings were getting colder and Helen and I fixed up a calor gas stove and an electric fire to heat the barn. By November these fires did not supply sufficient warmth so we both sat in our fur coats with blankets over our knees.

Then torrential rain began to find the weak parts of the roof of the barn, consequently buckets and bowls were placed around to catch the drips. Here the two of us sat in our glory, watching television. Eventually some of the rooms in the house were ready for decorating. At last we could use the kitchen for cooking and sitting to eat our meals.

However, on December 19th, just when I had hoped to enjoy a little more comfort, disaster struck. Mart, the carpet fitter arrived to lay some of the carpets in the bathroom and bedrooms. I asked him if he would like some apples. He was delighted and accepted the offer. Off I went and erected a ladder up to the apple store. It was snowing hard and Helen was sweeping the snow away from the back door when suddenly she heard a crash. Unfortunately the ladder was partly exposed to the elements and as I climbed up it crashed to the ground. No doubt the snow was the cause of its slipping. With two broken ankles I walked at least fifteen yards to the back door. Suddenly I became very dazed and to Helen and Mart it became apparent that an ambulance had to be sent for. It was not long before it arrived and I was taken to hospital where both legs were put in plaster. I was in hospital for three days before I was sent home, or rather to my son John and his wife Jennifer's home. On Christmas Day I was transported to visit my other son Cedric and his wife Lynda for the day.

The plasters on my legs became most irritating and I was then taken to the clinic where new plasters were put on and I remained there for ten days. Then I returned home to Newtown Linford and went from room to room in a wheel chair.

This went on until the plasters were removed after eight weeks of being immobile. Men were still putting the finishing touches to the house. Whilst Helen was away at school during the day the men would prepare sandwiches and make the tea or coffee for me, but the laugh came when they had an S.O.S. to wheel me to the toilet.

The brick layer was very helpful. A new fridge was to be installed under the working surfaces in the kitchen, so he brought the Volvo estate car to the back door, wheeled me to the car and lifted me into the front seat. My wheel chair was put into the back,and off the two of us went into Leicester. Once there I was lifted out of the car and put into the wheel chair and taken into a store to purchase a fridge.

Whilst I was convalescing I began to think seriously of moving back to Rothley where Reg had taken me to live after the war.

nine
RETURN to ROTHLEY

*M*any years ago, when Reg and I lived in Rothley and before purchasing the Paddocks, we went to look at a 16th century cottage in the village, near to the church, which came on the market but which was not suitable for us at that time. It was very beautiful, each room heavily beamed, one room having a massive inglenook fireplace in it. The gardens were a great feature – lawns, apple trees and rambling roses, bush roses, complete with a lovely archway of evergreens which led to the garage.

In my heart I knew that this cottage would now be ideal for me, amongst the friends I had left behind and also close to the shops.

How very strange that some weeks later this cottage was up for sale. I could not wait to see it once more, so I telephoned a friend to see if she could transport me there. By this time I was walking with two sticks so I was reasonably mobile.

When I saw the cottage again I realised that somehow I had to work on selling the house at Newtown Linford, and purchase this property. I contacted the agent who was selling it and he came out to view my property, whereupon he convinced me that he had a buyer wanting a property of this description. It was almost too good to be true. The man in question was actually a well known builder and on his first visit he came along with his architect. Over a cup of tea he remarked that he wished to buy the property and would pay the price I had stated.

Apparently he had been looking for a property like this for many weeks and was beginning to despair when his mother mentioned to him that her best friend a clairvoyant was paying a visit and so persuaded him to have a seance with her. At this time he had not even seen the Newtown Linford property but she said, "In ten days time you will find the property you are looking for." She explained it in great detail even to the house and cow sheds and barns, stone-built with Swithland slate roofs, at the foot of a hill and with a stream running through the property.

After contracts were duly signed the builder told me about this episode and he made his offer so quickly in case another purchaser came along. The strange thing about it was he wanted to view the property as soon as the estate agent informed him of it, but I had flatly refused at the time, as it was most inconvenient owing to my injuries and my having, strangely enough, to learn to walk again after the plasters were removed from my legs. As it so happened I decided on a date which turned out to be the tenth day, as the clairvoyant had stated, although of course I was unaware of this.

So I purchased the cottage at Rothley and this builder was very kind and sent me some of his men to help with the alterations which had to be carried out before I could move in.

In the year 1977 I met a widower by the name of Eric in an antique shop in the village of Desford, where I would from time to time make a visit to purchase antiques for re-sale.

Right from this first meeting we seemed to be attracted to each other. It did not take him long to find out where I lived and to contact me suggesting he visit me. As we talked I realised we had much in common. He too had lost his beloved wife from cancer, and together we have shared our grief. His visits became more frequent and eventually he proposed to me. I accepted and he bought me a beautiful sapphire ring.

In January of 1978 we were married. Neither of us will ever forget the morning of the wedding. A white Rolls Royce had been ordered to take Eric and me, Helen, the Best Man and his wife to the Registry Office in Leicester.

Time was running out and there was no sign of this car, so the Best Man telephoned the garage and was told that the booking had not been entered into their appointment book. The garage owner said that we were not to worry and a car would be on its way. Presently there came a knock at the door and I was aghast when I saw a man standing there who announced, "Your car is waiting". There he was in working clothes when naturally I was expecting a uniform and a cap. The next shock was the car – a bit of a banger. There were three cars standing in our drive, but it never occurred to us to send this man away and take one of our own cars!

Helen and Valerie squeezed in the front passenger seat, and Eric, Gort and I in the back. It's at times like these you look around hoping the neighbours aren't looking. Well, what a journey. At one set of traffic lights the car almost conked out, and it looked as if we should have to get out and push. But luckily we made it to the Registry Office. Can you imagine the Bride in all her glory, dressed in a beautiful long pale grey silk suit, complete with a lovely grey fox fur cape draped around her shoulders, stepping out of this banger! We just scurried into the Registry Office, the Best Man making sure that this man and his banger did not return to pick us up after the ceremony. Instead he ordered a first class taxi to take us to the Hotel for the Wedding Breakfast.

We had only been married a short time when Eric's mother had a fall. She broke her hip and had to be rushed to hospital. Once she was discharged she came to live with us, while her house was being altered, installing a downstairs bedroom and bathroom. Once this was completed she returned to her home amongst her old friends.

One day when Eric and I paid her a visit we met several of her friends and amongst them was a little old lady called Flossie. During the conversation, and as it was nearing Valentine's Day, she remarked that she had never received a Valentine card. So I immediately went into action. I bought a card, also a beautiful pair of fancy red garters. I packed these up and sent them off to my sister-in-law Olive in Lowestoft, to post them on from there thus avoiding any signs of a Leicester post mark. However Flossie never divulged this little secret not even to Eric's mother to whom she was very attached.

Eric's mother, in spite of her age, was a dear lady and still retained an interest in some of the finer qualities of life, looking after her well being and her wonderful choices of clothes. Unfortunately she never really recovered from that first fall and it was not long before she had another, and slowly and peacefully passed away.

Eric is very interested in aeroplanes of all descriptions. He and his "buddies" meet up from time to time to reminisce on their activities during the Second World War. During this war Eric was on maintenance at the Desford Flying Training School. Afterwards this school was disbanded, and he remained at the T.I. (Tubes) Desford until his retirement. I find his experiences whilst at Desford Flying Training School very interesting as this brings back memories, some sad and some happy, of those early war years in 1941, being so near to the Lincolnshire Aerodromes.

In October of 1980 Eric and I decided to take a holiday. Fortunately for us one of his friends offered us the loan of her villa in Denia in Spain. This was too good an offer to refuse. As Helen was on holiday from school we invited her to go along too. She drove the Volvo to Heathrow Airport and then continued in the car which was awaiting our arrival in Spain. The villa was in a lovely setting, in its own grounds with other villas surrounding it, only five minutes from the sea and beach.

But oh dear! The weather was so unkind to us. That year most other countries suffered likewise. At night the wind and rain rattled the shutters, reminding me of the story of Wuthering Heights. It felt really spooky. After all we were the only residents. The other owners had closed their villas for the winter.

The following evening when we returned to the villa after at least enjoying a meal at an English restaurant some two miles away, as we opened the door what did we see? A gecko climbing up the wall. Both Helen and I shrieked out to Eric, "Kill it, kill it". But by that time it had crept through a little hole in the ceiling and disappeared. I did not sleep well that night. This creature could have returned from its hiding place to creep under our bedroom door!

On our return the next evening there it was again, but this time coolly reposing on the settee. Helen and I took a closer look and really we had to admire its beauty. By this time we withdrew our request to kill it and asked Eric to gently pick it up and put it outside.

Whilst walking along the beach one day we met a German and his wife. We sat on some rocks and talked for quite a while. Suddenly the German stood up and announced that he was going to take a swim.

He swam a little way out but then suddenly stood up and delved into his swimming trunks and produced a long pink thing. He then put it back into his trunks. Eric, Helen and I looked up at each other in utter amazement lifting our eyebrows at the same time. His wife sat there and said nothing.

When he returned he stood near to his wife and again put his hand into his trunks and pulled out a thermometer. After all that the laugh was on us. Apparently before his wife took a swim the water had to be a certain temperature. Still he could have warned us about his thermometer, instead of having us guessing. We still talk and laugh about this unusual incident.

In spite of the weather being so cheerless we would take our daily walk along the beach. One day on our way back we decided to explore the intriguing holiday complex known as the Pueblo. This provided a selection of holiday homes built on two storeys in the style of an old Spanish Fishing Village. It captured the atmosphere of time gone by with its irregularly constructed facades with sloping roofs. By passing under an arched portico one had access to a beautiful inner courtyard. Here one had the feeling of being in a walled garden, the focal point being a fountain, roses climbing up the balconies with added tubs of beautiful plants thus making it a most enchanting feature.

We were all awed by finding such hidden beauty within this quaint setting, when an object which was out of character caught my eye. It was a box. Slowly I approached it and flicked back the lid. To my horror I saw a half eaten rat. But this carcase was not the only occupant of the box. Cuddled up together were three little kittens fast asleep. Eric and Helen came across to take a peep whereupon we decided to take our leave and go off and purchase some cat food. Suddenly mother cat came into the courtyard giving out a very concerned Miaow. We left immediately rather than lingering to distress her and her family.

Later on we returned with some food, but mother cat was already planning her next move. When I opened the shutters the following morning there she was playing on the patio with her three kittens. We allowed them in for a short time but decided to act with caution. Somehow we had to consider how we could provide shelter for them.

Nearby another complex was being built. After the men left in the evening Eric wandered off there and returned with an old drum. It was not long before we made them a bed by splitting up a cardboard box and laying a towel on the top and putting this inside the drum. Before we left to return to England we hid the drum in some bushes to protect mother and kittens from the storms. It was very heart rending to leave them but there was no other choice.

Eric and I lived in the cottage in Rothley until 1985. This was when I realised that my daughter Helen was slowly losing her sight. Everything was done to try and find out why, even going to see a specialist in Harley Street in London, but to no avail.

It was obvious that she would have to give up teaching. This concerned me greatly. Then I had an idea. Along the road a house came up for sale, in fact a house that I had had my eye on when Reg was still alive. Something had to be done to give Helen an interest to help her recover from the shock of losing some of her sight. As she had taught pottery at night school this seemed to me to be the answer. I talked it over with Helen and she was delighted at the suggestion of having her own little business, so I negotiated the purchase of this house which is called Sorrel House. On moving in I purchased a potter's wheel and kiln and Helen set to work along with her friends Will and Heather. They would go to craft fairs and sell their wares. However, sad to say after some months Helen's sight deteriorated so much she couldn't carry on. The kiln and the potter's wheel became silent. Helen was by now registered blind.

Some years later she had a brain scan in a hospital in London and was found to have Multiple Sclerosis. This was a great shock to her and to myself and also to Helen's very dear friend Jill who that very evening had taken us in her car to visit the specialist to hear the result of the scan. Jill was indeed a tower of strength to the two of us.

That night Helen returned to her own home and I to mine. I was absolutely devastated. My thoughts were with her all night long. Sleep was out of the question. I prayed as I have never prayed before in my life. The following evening I am convinced my prayers were answered. I went off to bed as usual and fell asleep but suddenly something woke me up. I could feel the presence of someone standing at my bedside although there was no one to be seen. From this spirit or phantom, or whatever stood there, a glow appeared and suddenly I could feel the warmth of someone caressing my shoulders. From then on I was convinced it was the spirit of her father. He had appeared to give me the support and strength I greatly needed at that time.

I remember an instance when Helen and I attempted to put up a bean fence in her kitchen garden. As we hammered away and the stakes refused to stand up straight Helen turned her face heavenwards and said, "If you are looking down Dad from up there then please lend us a hand". Eventually we made a good job of the fence. But Helen has been very brave and enjoys life to the full whenever her disability allows.

Over a period of years Helen's sight fluctuated even to her being able to attend a coure in audio typing at the R.N.I.B. College which opened in Loughborough at that time. All seemed to be going well, then the shadow of tragedy struck her as she wended her way, with the aid of her white stick, to meet a friend in Loughborough. She felt as if her lights had been switched off, and that a fog had descended around her. She was terrified and had no idea of her whereabouts. Eventually her friend found her, hailed a taxi, and brought her home. This ordeal completely shattered her confidence.

On the advice of a very dear friend who is employed at the Queen's Medical Centre, Nottingham, an appointment was made with an eminent neuroligist, who then recommended a secon opinion from an ophthalmologist.

It seemed that after all the barriers Helen had faced, she had now found her way through. From then onwards she attended Moorfields Hospital, London, where professor Susan Lightman was able to offer a unique operation, which had a 50-50 chance of success. At this stage in Helen's life her sight was so poor she felt she had nothing to losein accepting the challenge. The first operation was performed on the left eye in November 1994, and had positive results in that some sight was restored.

In April the following year a second operation was performed at the same hospital, by the very same surgeon, Mr Hamish Towler, with the same outcome. How wonderful – Helen's lights were once again switched on.

So it was that when the Gulf War broke out this was inevitably the therapy that I needed. I took it upon myself to write letters out to the 9/12 Royal Lancers.

Once the men of the Leicestershire Regiment, the 9/12 Royal Lancers, were posted out to the Gulf, the well known Leicester Mercury established a front line posting campaign.

Each evening at least three names, with ranks, photos and hobbies, were published and the readers were requested to take up their pens and write to these men to let them know they were not forgotten.

The first weekend I wrote three letters. I looked at the photo of this young boy, only seventeen years of age, serving on H.M.S. Gloucester. My heart went out to him and I felt I wanted to send him a token of good luck. The only thing that came into my mind was a piece of white heather. Although it was snowing at the time, I went into the garden to pluck some heather to dry and press it before putting it into his letter.

The next one was to someone who did not like animals. At first I thought I couldn't write to someone who did not like animals, but on second thoughts I decided that in spite of this he too was fighting for freedom. Then I took out my photo album and chose a photo of a lovely little calf I had reared and sent this to him. At the same time I told him to visit me on his return from the Gulf, as I hoped to change his attitude to some of the delightful creatures, especially the lovely pink pigs with their coats like pure silk. What a disappointment! He never replied.

The third letter was to a Sergeant who as a lad had lived not far from where I had once resided. So it was that this Sergeant somewhere out in the desert shed a tear or two after reading a letter from home. It was only one of the thousands being sent from people in Leicestershire, but in this instance it was the one I had written to him. In his reply he said, "I want to thank you from the bottom of my heart for your letter and photo. Myself and the rest of the Troop are deeply moved." The photo in question was of my brother Edgar, one of the first Desert Rats serving out in the desert in 1942. This I hoped he would carry with him at all times and then bring it back safely to England.

My writing continued and I received many lovely replies. Suddenly the shops were ablaze with Valentine Cards. I endeavoured to send each soldier a card. Then whilst I was choosing a special card for the Sergeant I saw a card with bears on it, whereupon I turned to my daughter Helen and said that this would be an ideal card for Storming Norman. Helen said, "You can't send him that". "Who can't", I replied and bought it immediately. The little bear said to the big bear, "Will you spend Valentine's Day with me?" So this card was posted to the Commander in Chief, Storming Norman Schwarzkoff, Operation Desert Storm, Riyadh, Saudi Arabia.

Somewhere out in the Desert stood a Grizzly Bear ready to swipe with his paw and to defend all that he believed in. Such was the case of Storming Norman (*the Bear* as he was known) closely examining the final details of his

Photo courtesy of Leicester Mercury

assault on Saddam's army in his bid for the freedom of Kuwait. Then for a few brief moments this powerful bear relaxed and opened his mail. Suddenly his face lit up as he reached out and looked at the Valentine Card, sent by me, of the two bears and he became another kind of bear, a much softer and warmer bear. It was obvious he appreciated my thoughts towards him as he sent the following letter, dated 18th February 1991, just six days before the ground attack began. There was a little spot in his heart I had reached.

Dear Mrs Neale

Thank you very much for your kind card. I deeply appreciate the tremendous support we are receiving from freedom loving citizens around the World. Cards with support like yours are exactly what our magnificent men and women need and deserve.

I was delighted that you asked me to share Valentine's Day with you. As you know, I was unavoidably detained at my post. However I think it should be me expressing admiration to you for being so spry at 73 years young.

Thank you again for taking time to write to me and express your support. God bless you.

Sincerely

N. Schwarzkoff

Somewhere, too out in the desert a young army nurse slept with her teddy bear, maybe her little friend of many years. She may have had a makeshift bed, her helmet at her side, yet she would be well aware that dawn might bring chemical injuries, burns and lost limbs and even death. Just for a short time, clutching the teddy bear she might fall into oblivion, so peaceful, almost like a child. Yet, somewhere too out in the desert a GI might befriend a young Iraqi boy comforting him with an arm around his shoulders and maybe a bar of chocolate in his pocket to give to him.

In these sandy wastes everyone was almost like an orphan of the storm, all miles away from their homes and families. They slept within reach of their helmets, gas masks, guns and tanks. Instead of friends they had comrades. Instead of homes they had tents. Instead of wives and girlfriends they had only letters. Thank Heaven for teddy bears, for making friends out of strangers and for the hands of friendship that reach out. Thank goodness for the pictures which prove that behind the bloodied scoreboard of war humanity survives.

Two friends of mine, nurses in a hospital in Riyadh, wrote me a letter telling me of an unusual sight they had seen. Amidst the turmoil of war they saw passing the window of the hospital a camel riding on the back of a Toyota pick up truck.

The planning for this war was going on for months in General Schwarzkoff's war room. Finally the Allied Commander in Chief drew a circle around February 24th on his calendar. The time was to be four o'clock in the morning when the moon would throw no light over the Iraqi troops who would be blinded without the night sight devices the 28 Nation Alliance possessed. It gave time to complete at least the heaviest fighting of Saddam's "Mother of Wars" before the sand storms came and the day time heat turned the desert into an open oven.

One last order from Storming Norman Schwarzkoff launched the land battle. News of the invasion was announced by an aide, his words were as follows, "The liberation of Kuwait has begun as planned".

Wearing his familiar battle fatigues Storming Norman strode into the press briefing room exuding confidence and flashes of his usual good humour and boomed out, "We're going to go around, over, through, on top, underneath and any way it takes to beat them". This great man showed no signs of stress and fatigue at the briefing in Riyadh just twelve hours after the start of the biggest land battle since the Second World War. At sea Amphibious missions were being carried out along the Kuwaiti Coast while Allied Warships bombarded the shore with gunfire.

The Coalition and the RAF aircraft supported the ground offensive by striking at the key strategic targets.

These troops had expected stiff resistance believing that the Iraqis would be well dug in and heavily armed, but it was just the opposite, most of the fox holes were empty. In the American section of the front US Marines smashed into Kuwait through Iraqi defensive lines within two hours. Amazingly, about 30 minutes after the invasion had begun the Marines just overran the first mine fields, barbed wire and other Iraqi defences, blasting them aside with concentrated fire.

The SAS had been the Allied secret weapon in the build up to the land war. These crack troops spread destruction and confusion behind enemy lines. They dressed as Arabs, spoke the Arab tongue and looked like Arabs.

The Nation's most decorated soldier, Sir Peter de la Billiere, was appointed as Britain's Gulf Commander. Everything we had was thrown at Saddam's front line. In fact Saddam's so called "wall of death" was little more than an obstacle course. Many of Saddam's troops had no stomach for a fight and his beaten men tore up their tattered clothes to use as flags of surrender.

The Gulf War, after one of the biggest military build ups since the Second World War was executed with devastating swiftness. Iraqi positions were pummelled relentlessly by coalition air men before a four day land offensive which drove Saddam Hussein from the ravaged emirate. War supremo General Norman Schwarzkoff eventually described the allied offensive to free Kuwait as a dramatic success.

Our Queen told aides she wanted to honour the General after watching in awe his briefings on TV. Eventually the Gulf hero was awarded a Honorary Knighthood by the Queen, at the US Army's Central Command Headquarters in Tampa Florida. It was a remarkable sight as the Queen is at least a foot shorter than Sir Storming Norman, and just came up to the four silver stars on the General's epaulettes. This was indeed a proud moment for Storming Norman as he received from the Queen a star and a badge as "Knight Commander of the Bath".

On November 11th 1992 a Squadron of the 9/12 Royal Lancers flew into what was Yugoslavia. They had for the last two months trained hard for the tough job of escorting and protecting convoys throughout the war-torn region. Many of the crack reconnaissance team were from Leicestershire. It was not long before some of these men came under mortar fire. They constantly ran the gauntlet along dangerous roads to deliver vital supplies of food and medicine to the cold, sick and hungry.

Once more I took up my pen to write to these brave soldiers. Bitter cold, driving rain and snow were just some of the conditions they had to endure in the winter months that lay ahead. Therefore it was vital for the people of Leicestershire to pen a few lines to boost the morale of these men. One can well imagine how lonely a man could be as he patrolled an isolated track. But to arrive back at camp and find letters awaiting must be very heart warming. In fact, in helping one side one becomes the enemy of the other, even though these troops are there solely on humane grounds.

One soldier serving along the mountain roads was eventually tracked down by army personnel to inform him he was the father to a lovely daughter who was christened Hannah Jane. Once I knew of this birth I immediately sent out a congratulatory card to him. He wrote back to me and expressed his appreciation of my kind thoughts on this happy occasion. On his return to base he received a rousing cheer from his mates but sad to say the only celebration drink on hand was a cup of Army Ration Tea.

As Christmas 1992 was drawing nigh I sat down and began a long list of names to send Christmas Cards. With each card I enclosed a typed version of the following song, hoping they could gather round on Christmas Day to sing it loud and clear:

There's something about a soldier
There's something about a soldier
There's something about a soldier
That is **FINE – FINE – FINE**

He may be a great big general
He may be a sergeant major
He may be a private
Of the **LINE – LINE – LINE**

There's something that he's wearing
There's something about his bearing
There's something about his buttons
All a **SHINE – SHINE – SHINE**

For the military chest
Seems to suit the ladies best
There's something about a soldier
That is **FINE – FINE – FINE**

Two of the girls from Leicestershire who were sent out to be the drivers to the officers were not afforded any special privileges. In fact the roof above the room where they slept began to leak. Considering the bitter winds and rain as they battled along I decided to send the two girls face cream and tissues as such weather plays havoc with one's skin. Just before Christmas I received a lovely card from one of the girls with the words, "The gifts of Christmas are many and beautiful, and of them all, the sweetest, the finest is truly the gift of love".

Captain Tim Hancock sent me a Christmas Card on which he wrote , *"Many thanks for all your letters, they are appreciated by all"*, Signed Tim Hancock and

all in B Squadron. On television, in the Review of the Year 1992 on December 29th, I saw myself on the screen writing to the soldiers out in Bosnia and sending Valentine Cards, in a recording made in February of that year.

Photo courtesy of Leicester Mercury

In the old days the area of Mostar was one of the most prosperous regions with pretty villages and farm houses, now the whole area has been brutalised. Sometimes one wonders if this humanitarian mission is as futile as trying to irrigate the Sahara with a watering can. After six months of these conditions it was natural that the 9/12 Lancers were glad to be relieved of their duties and sent back to Germany and to England.

Friends of mine were going on a week's holiday on a narrow boat and invited me along. I was delighted to accept their invitation. This couple were in their forties and I was approaching 74 years. On Saturday June 29th 1991 Andrew and Barbara and their two children Matthew and Rachel and I set off to Alvechurch Boat Yard in Birmingham. A six berth narrow boat named "The Snipe" was ready and waiting for us. After a technical briefing we left the yard at about 3.30 p.m. on our 86 mile journey.

You actually see a whole new world afloat when you are down at the eye level of wild birds and water fowl. This kind of holiday gives one the freedom of just drifting through meadows and tranquil villages, gliding beneath bridges and overhanging trees. The pace is leisurely and the mood carefree and everyone you meet is so friendly whatever the nationality.

Rachel and I walked two miles on that first afternoon opening and shutting the lock gates but we enjoyed every minute of it. At 8 o'clock that first evening we moored the boat at Oozell Street Loop for the night.

On Sunday morning we were up for a bright and early breakfast, then went on our way once more. It is unbelievable the amount of locks we encountered. On that day we negotiated a total of 21, in what is called the Wolverhampton Flight, but not without mishaps. Matthew all but fell overboard, and Rachel lost the precious windlass in the canal much to the disgust of her father. Fortunately two were provided and along the route we purchased another.

The next day we travelled through seventeen locks then moored the boat when we approached a gift shop, where we could take on water. Here I purchased for Andrew the Captain's badge, and for Barbara the Second Mate, but they presented me with the badge that said "General Dogsbody". We were a very good team – the Captain was in charge of The Snipe, Barbara was the cook, and the children and I were in charge of preparing the vegetables and doing the washing up. We took it in turns to steer the boat.

On one particularly sunny day the Captain decided to moor the boat so that they could all sunbathe on the roof. He apologised to me as he thought I would not be able to get on to that part of the boat, but he was not aware of what was going on in my mind. Once they were all settled I fetched a stool and clambered up to join them, much to the amazement of them all.

At Stourport we went off to the shops to purchase provisions and to have afternoon tea – strawberries and cream at the Tudor Tea Rooms.

By the Wednesday our captain decided to branch off and travel along the River Severn, then back on to the Birmingham-Worcester Canal. We had a lovely lunch in Worcester and visited the Porcelain Museum and Shop. I watched with great interest as a member of staff was escorting a renowned couple who evidently were choosing most costly articles of Porcelain. They were a handsome couple, she smiled sweetly at me. Her Oriental attire was absolutely gorgeous. It was obvious they were very rich. Among their purchases was a huge vase on a mahogany plinth, a most expensive item. Tea in the Guild Hall Assembly Rooms was delightful, with classical music on a grand piano. Back to the boat and more locks – sixteen this time. We had a bet as to who could steer the boat into the lock with the least bumps. None of us really excelled ourselves on this.

On Friday we had to start our return to the boat yard via another 30 locks and two tunnels. That night we had dinner at the Queens Head Restaurant, where everyone met for the last meal of the holiday before handing the boats back for 12 noon on the Saturday.

This was a wonderful holiday and I would recommend narrow boating to everyone.

Although progress is necessary in every part of the country, in spite of the new buildings being erected in Rothley there still remains much of interest and beauty here. The old granite church, founded in Norman days has a massive 15th Century tower with nave and aisles a century or two older.

Hidden away in its high walled grounds stands Rothley Temple, where in 1800 that great statesman and man of letters, Thomas Babington Macauley was born whilst his mother, a Babington, was visiting family. The room in which he was born, with its fine 18th Century panelling is little changed today. Lord Macauley was very fond of Rothley and carried out a good deal of his writing here.

In 1231 Henry III granted the manor and grounds to the Knights Templar and they established a community (known as a preceptory) shortly thereafter. Their chapel was built next to the existing Manor House around 1240. This is now considered second only to the Temple in London as the best preserved Templar Chapel in Britain. When the Templars were abolished in the early 14th Century having become too powerful for the comfort of the French King, Rothley Temple and its possessions passed to the Knights of St John of Jerusalem, who leased out the land for farming. In 1536 Humphrey Babington took on a lease and in 1565 his son Thomas bought the estate outright. The Babingtons were lords of the manor and land of Rothley for nearly 300 years.

In 1845 the Babingtons sold the estate to an in-law Sir James Parker whose son married the daughter of Kitchener of Khartoum. In fact it was whilst on a visit to the house that Lord Kitchener was summoned to his campaign in Egypt.

Rothley Temple remained a private home until the 1930's when for some years it was run as a nursing home. I visited an elderly relation there, her bedroom was possibly the one that Lord Macauley was born in.

Then in 1950 the late Clive Wormleighton (a local man) bought the house, chapel and remaining 6 acres of land and converted it into a hotel and restaurant in 1960, laying the foundation of what is now Rothley Court.

Anyone wishing to visit the chapel may do so by requesting the key at the reception desk.

January 1994 marked the 25th Anniversary of the Main Line Preservation Group. Whilst most businesses are still feeling the effects of the recession the Great Central Line is fortunately going from strength to strength. The return of the steam trains attracts many thousands of enthusiasts to Rothley.

Over the last twenty five years there has always been a great team of volunteers, staff and management. These railways are run by enthusiasts who, whilst they are now successful people, may have been the grubby train spotters of forty or so years ago. Those train spotters have developed into professional steam railway operators over the ensuing years.

There has been a lot of hard work, many ups and downs, and no doubt disagreements. But success has been achieved to the extent that this line, running from Loughborough through Rothley Station to Leicester North, is considered to be unique amongst preserved railways.

Large Locomotives such as the 7029 Clun Castle, the 34030 Boscastle, the 35005 Canadian Pacific, the famous A4 Pacific N04493 Sir Nigel Gresley as well as the well turned out rolling stock and extending the line to Leicester, are good publicity and all this helps in bringing the Railway greater fame and success. A successful share issue has enabled works to be undertaken using the funds raised. Furthermore a scene from the film "Shadowlands", popular both in America and in England, was filmed on Loughborough Station.

ten
SUNSET

*M*any miles I have travelled along life's highway being greatly touched by the seasons. Life is like a garden, apart from attaining great pleasure in creating a beautiful garden, I have also unearthed a great amount of history in the garden of my life, of people, experiences and growth.

Now reaching the autumn of my life I can look back, reflect upon all that has happened, having passed through 79 Springs, 79 Summers, 79 Autumns and 79 Winters.

Over the past twelve months I have found great pleasure in restoring an old confectioner's hand cart which originally travelled the streets of Horncastle. Perhaps the owner all those years ago could be heard calling out, "hot cross buns", especially on Good Friday, which still remains a tradition to this day. I recently negotiated a sale of this cart to a very old firm of florists in the town of Horncastle as I felt it should return from whence it came. This morning I received the following cutting out of the Horncastle News;

Carted Off

A Victorian confectioner's handcart which used to ply its trade in Horncastle Market Place has returned to its Lincolnshire roots. Crowders Nurseries bought the cart from Dorothy Neale (79), who now lives in Leicester but was born in Kirkby-on-Bain and whose parents came from Horncastle. The cart has been restored and given a bright new livery by Crowders.

It is the little things that mean alot. Too much time is spent on material things. The greed and power of man destroys much of the beauty in this lovely world of ours as well as terrible suffering and pain.

There is far greater pleasure to be obtained from listening to the dawn chorus of the birds, watching the butterflies as they flit from flower to flower, even to hear a new born baby cry, to his or her first tooth and most of all watching those first unsteady steps on their pathway of life.

Going back many years I remember so well standing on the bridge over the River Bain which meandered on its way through my father's fields, watching the black shiny moorhens, busily pecking away as they swam along near to the water's edge. An occasional rat would show itself, then down would come a most beautiful lonesome heron, diligently waiting for its prey. Once it caught a fish away it flew with it in its beak.

A wild stray black cat crossed a busy street, passing many houses on her way, yet she chose us, suddenly appearing with three little kittens early one Saturday morning. All wild. For a temporary home my husband and I put a tea chest amongst the trees. She was a lovely mother. Each evening at about seven o'clock she brought the kittens out into the garden, they had a lovely time climbing the trees. At times one would get a 'wham' with her paw. Seems even in animal life mother corrects her family. Eventually they all became tame. Helen, my daughter, had the three kittens, Emma (the tortoiseshell), Felix (the beautiful black one with his white dickey bow) and Chalky (the white one with black markings) and we kept mother, Sooty. Oh! the joy from such little things.

In later years when I came to live in Leicestershire my first home was opposite to a cherry orchard. The blossom was absolutely magnificent, followed by scrumptious glistening dark red cherries. Alas! the trees have long since gone, replaced by houses and bungalows.

One particular scene comes to mind of mother duck crossing the lawn, followed by six ducklings on their way to the pond in the corner of the field, all happily quacking away. Lambs too, are very interesting as you watch them play. Strange though it may seem if you wait long enough you will realise that one little lamb becomes the overseer, so whatever he or she does the others follow suit, just like children really. When I lived at Newtown Linford the River Lyn travelled through my garden. Sometimes a Kingfisher would appear as it skimmed over the stream, the lovely blue plummage reflected in the water.

During the winter of the Gulf war a blue grey cat appeared in Helen's garden looking miserable, thin and unwanted. I adopted this cat, and with love, care and attention he soon responded and turned out to be a very fine animal. Names have really got to suit an animal, so can you guess? of course, I called him Norman after Storming Norman. Like him the cat is big, strong, handsome and most of all very intelligent.

Wherever I roam nature surrounds me. Even in the Autumn of my life I can look across the road to the fields beyond and watch the rabbits having a lovely time, occasionally sitting up on their hind legs, pricking up their ears, maybe listening to the footsteps of their enemy – man.

During the winter months my husband and I put out nuts for the birds. One day we saw a squirrel hanging upside down on the wire container of nuts having a jolly good feed. He became very friendly and would take nuts from our fingers.

Eventually we gave him the name of Sid. To our surprise one day "Sid" appeared on the fence followed by three baby squirrels. In spite of this we could not think of changing her name. It had to remain Sid. It was most interesting watching her swish her bushy tail which appeared to be a signal to her babies as the "All clear" for them to come down off the fence and onto the bird table to feed. They were all very partial to grapes. A pretty sight to behold – four squirrels sitting on their hind legs each holding a grape in their front paws.

Sadly the other day I witnessed a most horrific incident, two male blackbirds were fighting to establish which of the two owned the territory when swiftly a hawk appeared, grabbed one in its beak, threw it to the ground, trampled on it and then flew off carrying it in its beak. They are all God's creatures but I would prefer it if this kind of predator did not visit my garden.

Here is one tradition that never changes. As the Autumn leaves begin to fall the children are out under the Chestnut trees looking for Conkers. All my life the wild geese have seemed to follow me almost as if it is the call of the wild as they fly overhead calling out, flying in formation as they disappear from view. Wherever I am and what ever the hour, I have to go to them and watch them. A strange feeling comes over me which I cannot explain.

The many things that I have recalled in my life's garden are very special and that is why the poem of Rudyard Kipling has always been a favourite of mine. In fact I recited it when I was eighteen years old on stage in a Methodist chapel. It now gives me great pleasure to record it at this time. For me this encapsulates all the beauty of a garden of a person's life and for me this England has been the place where my life's garden has been.

The Glory of the Garden

Our England is a garden that is full of stately views,
Of borders, beds and shrubberies and lawns and avenues,
With statues on the terraces and peacocks strutting by;
But the glory of the garden lies in more than meets the eye.

For where the old thick laurels grow, along the thin red wall,
You find the tool- and potting-sheds which are the art of all;
The cold-frames and the hot-houses, the dung pits and the tanks,
The rollers, carts and drain pipes with the barrows and the planks.

And there you'll see the gardeners, the men and 'prentice boys
Told off to do as they are bid and do it without noise;
For, except when seeds are planted and we shout to scare the birds,
The Glory of the Garden it abideth not in words.

And some can pot begonias and some can bud a rose,
And some are hardly fit to trust with anything that grows;
But they can roll and trim the lawns and sift the sand and loam,
For the Glory of the Garden occupieth all who come.

Our England is a garden, and such gardens are not made,
By singing:– "Oh how beautiful!" and sitting in the shade,
While better men than we go out and start their working lives
At grubbing weeds from gravel-paths with broken dinner-knives.

There's not a pair of legs so thin, there's not a head so thick,
There's not a hand so weak and white, nor yet a heart so sick,
But it can find some needful job that's crying to be done,
For the Glory of the Garden glorifieth every one.

Then seek your job with thankfulness and work till further orders,
If it's only netting strawberries or killing slugs on borders;
And when your back stops aching and your hands begin to harden,
You will find yourself a partner in the Glory of the Garden.

Oh! Adam was a gardener, and God who made him sees
That half a proper gardener's work is done upon his knees,
So when your work is finished, you can wash your hands and pray
For the Glory of the Garden, that it may not pass away!
And the Glory of the Garden it shall never pass away!

Rudyard Kipling

After twenty years absence I had this desire to visit the village of my birth. During the lifetime of my brother Edgar, Reg and I would visit him and his wife Olive regularly. Then Edgar passed away and Olive moved back to her birth place of Oulton Broad in Suffolk to be near her relations, and so these visits came to an end. Andrew our friend for many years kindly chauffeured both my daughter Helen and myself to visit Ron and Betty Dixon who were friends of Edgar and Olive. Once they were aware of this visit they invited us to partake of coffee, scones and mince pies.

We set off early and our first port of call was to see Betty and Ron. After we had refreshed ourselves they both escorted us to the village school where Betty is secretary and general organiser.

The headmaster, a young man for such responsibility, welcomed us warmly, happy to reminisce over times gone by and to show us the many alterations to the layout of the building. A great transformation had taken place since I had left the village in 1946. Gone were the two old Combustion stoves with the tortoises moulded onto the lids, the big old iron fire guard, the large oil painted maps which covered all the walls, the main oak door now bricked up, the two seater desks with their ink wells, the beautiful old globe, the wall removed to the girls cloakroom adding extra space to the classroom where I spent my first days as a child and also where I taught the infants when I left school at the age of fifteen years The housing to the village clock remained and the clock is still in perfect working condition. It was a delight to hear the school bell calling the children back to their classes. To meet the demand of influx of children from the out lying villages it was obvious that further extensions had to be built.

We said farewell to the headmaster and his staff making our way down the narrow lane along side the hedgerows, where once Miss Logan had cut her canes, towards the church. On entering the gates of the church yard it was noticeably well kept, apparently due to the efforts of Ron during the summer months. One day as he was clearing away some tall undergrowth he came across a curious headstone, the inscription on this being, "*Louise Glen died 18th day of April 1939*" Strange though it may seem, on investigating none of the parishioners had heard of her, except Bill Spikings who owns the farm where I was born. He was one of the bearers of her coffin, called upon at the last minute when one of the bearers was taken ill. All he remembers was the fact that the coffin was extremely heavy. At the time it was rumoured this lady was buried in her wedding dress and that her coffin was lead lined. She and her husband apparently originated from York yet no one knows who they were and this still remains a mystery. The monument although some what damaged was of an expensive design. The husband must have loved his wife dearly.

We then entered the wire gate into the church porch, and towards the oak door beyond. This was a very nostalgic moment for me. The children's corner remained untouched – even the wool rug we all helped to make was still in good condition. As I walked down the aisle towards the altar memories came flooding back of when I walked on the arm of my late father to become a bride. This proved all too much. I was very upset, it was very difficult to retain my composure. All went quiet, it was obvious to all present of my emotions and they waited for me to speak once more.

My next visit was to the farmhouse where I was born. Bill and his wife Joyce made me very welcome and we thoroughly enjoyed reminiscing over the memories of yester years. On saying my farewell Bill's last words were don't make it another twenty years before you visit us again as I am sure I shall not be here. What a laugh – the two of us would be in our hundredth year.

From there I could not pass the post office without having a chat with Phyllis (Bill's sister) who had been the postmistress for many years and still continues at the ripe old age of 82 years.

The village itself was totally changed, new properties popping up every where. For instance one is in my late fathers' kitchen garden, another in the paddock beyond. The access to the river at the end of this road was closed, now part of someone's garden. This plot of ground is what is called "common ground" which really belongs to the villagers, where for years they could take their water-butts on wheels, and buckets, to collect water from the river.

Travelling through the village we came across yet another piece of "common ground", which is also fenced off. This was the water hole where the farmers could take their animals to drink, also where as children we walked the stepping stones as well as fishing under them. My father and another farmer could take their cattle and horse drawn vehicles to the fields they owned beyond. I remember the time when I drove the cows down to the water hole before taking them onto the field we called the "Rushie Field", no doubt because a small area was swampy. During the early summer months it was a joy to behold, the masses of colour of the flowers, red of the "Ragged Robin", the bright yellow of the large "King Buttercups," and the dainty mauve, pinky white flowers of the "Ladies Smocks". Mention of these fields brings to my mind the mole traps my brothers used to set, of the skins being stretched out on a board to dry for which each skin they received the sum of six pence. Thank goodness this is a thing of the past !

Time now to leave the village to travel on to Woodhall Spa, passing the forest area that housed the many different regiments of the second world war years, a quick look at the Kinema in the Woods, past the present tea- rooms, more elaborate than the smaller lesser building I once knew, and lastly the memorial to the Dambusters.

Next we travelled onto Horncastle as I wished to visit the garden centre owned by Crowders on the Lincoln road. This firm had purchased my hand cart. Leaving there we motored back towards Kirkby-on-Bain on the main road towards Coningsby, where I visited my last remaining friend Hilda, who sadly was quite unwell.

Driving back towards Leicestershire I was aware that Helen and Andrew were very quiet, no doubt realising that I wished to be alone with my own thoughts of the day's events. The one thing that captivated my imagination during the day was the epitaph inscribed on the grave of Louise Glen. To me this is a beautiful piece of poetry. It is almost like a fairy story catching something magical. Even going back reminding me of my own life too. It was like sweet music to my ears. and the essence of something that I can hold dearly to me for the rest of my life giving inspiration to others when they read the following words:

The sun, the birds and the trees
Soft wind and green leaves
If heaven holds but this for you and others
You will be happy.